Church at a Crossroads

Church at a Crossroads
Being the Church after Christendom

D. NEAL MACPHERSON

Foreword by Douglas John Hall

WIPF & STOCK · Eugene, Oregon

CHURCH AT A CROSSROADS
Being the Church after Christendom

Copyright © 2008 D. Neal MacPherson. All rights reserved. Except for brief quotations in critical publications or reviews, no part of this book may be reproduced in any manner without prior written permission from the publisher. Write: Permissions, Wipf and Stock, 199 W. 8th Ave., Suite 3, Eugene, OR 97401.

www.wipfandstock.com

ISBN 13: 978-1-55635-284-3

Manufactured in the U.S.A.

For Leilani

and the Members and Friends

of Church of the Crossroads

Contents

Foreword ix

Preface xvii

1. The Church in Context 1

2. The Shaping of a Church 29

3. Engaging the World 54

4. Our Stories at the Foot of the Cross 80

5. Gathered for Worship 105

6. The Spirit of Crossroads 129

   Bibliography 155

Foreword

BY DOUGLAS JOHN HALL, C.M.

As the author of numerous books and articles on the subject of the Christian Movement after the end of Christendom, I am very often (sometimes none too politely!) asked, "But what would the church look like if it suited *your* ideas?" I confess that I used to waffle in the face of that question sometimes. It's hard for theologians, who must work in the world of ideas, to become instant experts on church planning and practice. For the most part, they probably shouldn't even try.

And then, a few years ago, I got to know *Church of the Crossroads* in (of all places!) Honolulu. Since then, I have frequently answered that annoying question very concretely by saying, "Well, let me tell you about a church I've become acquainted with. . . ."

In 1999, three remarkable women showed up at Chautauqua, where I was speaking that year, and asked me if I would consider coming to their church in Hawai'i as "theologian-in-residence." I would be one in a line of such, they said (John Cobb, Jr. was certainly a name I knew), and they felt that my approach to the Christian faith might be compatible, in some basic way, with the kind of thing their community had been attempting. Perhaps they also sensed that I needed a "base-community" in which to anchor my own maybe-too-theoretical thought! In any case, I eventually accepted the challenge.

Since my first stint as theologian-in-residence at the Church of the Crossroads, six weeks in duration, I have returned on two occasions for somewhat shorter periods, and I am in touch with many members of the church, as well as its splendid pastor, the author of this book, on a regular basis.

There are, of course, many other instances of what I hope the church of the post-Christendom era will look like. In fact, more and more Christian communities have sprung up in the past few decades to explore

Foreword

the meaning and mission of the Christian Movement in this new religious situation that has come to be in the West—this strange new world in which "religion" is no longer a laid-on commodity and the old denominations of once-proud Christendom flounder and try to find out how they can survive. As Christendom dies, real *Christianity,* which, as Chesterton said, has been "so little tried," looks for a way into the future. And wherever Christians are serious enough to let go of the tired old forms their religion has assumed in its long and established past, they are discovering the courage and imagination necessary to put the good wine of the gospel into new ecclesiastical wineskins. Some of these wineskins will no doubt burst. Some already have. But some will survive and will prove sources of energy, wisdom, and human hope for the century ahead.

The Church of the Crossroads, in my belief, is one of the latter. But whether or not it survives *as* such—that is, as this church in this place and this particular form using this particular building, and so on—is not what matters. What matters, rather, is that this community has grasped some of the fundamental principles that—in my opinion, at any rate—must inform any Christian *koinonia* that hopes to weather the immense winnowing process, the *disestablishment* or *de-Constantinianization,* that has been under way in Christendom for the past two centuries or more, and that will continue and grow apace despite the statistical ups and downs of religion in the Western world generally and America particularly.

Let me name some of those principles, illustrating them very briefly by reference to the Church of the Crossroads as I know it. In this fine book, Neal MacPherson will provide the necessary details.

First, a Christian congregation needs and ought to welcome *diversity.* The name "Crossroads" is not just a name, it describes a very lively reality. As one would suppose of a church in Hawai'i (though it is not always found there), this congregation reflects the meeting of East and West that these islands uniquely facilitate. That meeting has not come about automatically or without pain. It's easy enough for liberal Christians to sing, "In Christ there is no east nor west . . . ," but especially during World War II and again during the Vietnam War, even Crossroaders had to learn that the kind of unity that grace makes possible "in Christ" is never altogether natural.

The diversity of the Church of the Crossroads, however, is not only racial and ethnic; it includes many other dimensions of human experience. There is a meeting of Christian denominations and of world religions—Buddhism, Islam, Hinduism, and others. The beautiful building in which the congregation meets features symbols of Shinto and other religious traditions, including Zoroastrianism (something I have never seen elsewhere). There is a meeting of academic, business, and professional worlds; a meeting of persons at the center of civic life and of those on the edges of the establishment; a meeting of straight and openly gay/lesbian people; a meeting of generations; a meeting of conservative and very liberal cultural, political, and theological mentalities; a meeting of social activists and more contemplative approaches to faith—I could go on. And what is so important about this diversity is that it is not hidden or merely assumed, as in many congregations; rather, it functions to enliven the whole discourse and social witness of the congregation. There is no one life-pattern or spiritual image that members of this community are expected to project. The unity of the congregation, which is certainly present and visible, does not devolve into uniformity. And isn't that what St. Paul is talking about in 1 Corinthians 12?

Second, a congregation that intends to fulfill its mission in the post-Christendom situation must *combine serious theological reflection with concrete engagement in its social context*. When I first appeared at Crossroads as theologian-in-residence, I assumed (on the basis of past experience with most congregations) that it would be necessary for me to explain even the most basic references to theological, historical, and scriptural matters. What a surprise it was to discover not only that significant numbers of people turned up for pretty "heavy" theological lectures and seminars, but that many of those present were unusually familiar with the concepts, terms, names, and basic concerns of traditional and contemporary theology. Some could correct me on my sometimes-too-general references to people like Barth and Rosemary Ruether and my teacher Paul Tillich! But the best part was the obvious enthusiasm and pleasure that rapt theological and scriptural discourse gave these people—I could have wished for something like it in seminary classes I have taught!

Yet this intellectual/spiritual engagement never became intellectualistic or pietistic, for it was combined with a profound and disciplined involvement in the social, cultural, and political life of its context. The very first thing my wife and I were invited to do, after my initial appearance before a theological study-group, was to walk in a protest march against the decision of the Bush administration to make war on Iraq—a large gathering of diverse groups in Honolulu, in which I suppose nearly half the congregation of Crossroads participated. The next day, we attended a day-long seminar about the struggle of indigenous Hawaiian peoples to maintain their history, culture, and identity in the face of the overwhelming commercial and cultural interests of the technological society. I have often experienced Christian communities in which the concern for peace and social justice is strong, and occasionally I have encountered congregations with serious theological and spiritual agendas, but the combination of the two—their creative interaction—is very, very rare.

Third, a Christian community which intends to take its stand in a world that is no longer automatically Christian or even religious needs to have among its numbers persons whose experience, education, and compassion equip them for *leadership*. I continue to be astonished at the array of expertise, concern, and commitment present in this community. No doubt the church's proximity to the University of Hawai'i and other educational institutions helps, but the leadership present at Crossroads goes beyond disciplines like medicine, history, geography, marine biology, literature, and others found in institutions of higher learning; it includes the sorts of worldly experience required for the understanding of and involvement in the great social and ethical issues of our time, everything from community health and the stewardship of resources to addictive gambling. A Christian community that can count upon informed and engaged persons to introduce its members and adherents to the realities and needs of their worldly context need never fear becoming a holy ghetto or ivory tower!

And here—though I know it will embarrass him—I cannot forebear mentioning the leadership of the minister himself. Neal MacPherson is the most modest clergyman I know, but his quiet, careful, and dedicated shepherding of the Crossroads congregation is certainly (in my opinion and that of many of his parishioners) one of the most salient reasons why this church is the exceptional Christian community that it is. From what I know of its history, Crossroads seems to have benefited from an exceptional number of extraordinary pastors over its eighty-plus years, and this again demonstrates—what hardly needs demonstrating!—the truth that good ministerial leadership makes all the difference. What a difference is made by the carefully thought-out sermons, the sensitive and often poetic public prayers, and the dignified yet ardent services of worship Neal prepares! With the help of very talented musicians, these services of

Foreword

worship are inspiring enough to sustain the work of the congregation and its diverse membership throughout the week.

The fourth principle that I would name as being essential to the life and work of the church today is, in fact, very hard to actually name. It has something to do with truth and mutuality and solidarity; it touches upon qualities like compassion, "attention" (in Simone Weil's sense)—attention to "the other"; it is a *practical* matter informing the day-to-day life of the community, yet it is also profoundly theological and scriptural. It will be best, I think, if I try to get at it indirectly by describing a prominent aspect of my experience of this community of discipleship.

We had not been present in Crossroads for more than a week or two before my wife and I began to notice something exceptional: As we got to know people a little, we heard story after story of personal suffering and the way in which that suffering had been met, shared, and in some real measure, healed within the fellowship of the church. A great variety of difficult, excruciating, and sometimes truly tragic experiences were told of—not only the all-too-common human fates of seemingly meaningless illness, accident, and death, but also more subtle agonies such as alienation, estrangement, stigmatization, injustice. We have both lived long enough to know that "bad things happen to good people." That was not the surprising factor here. What we began to notice was that the experience of suffering seemed an important link between the persons of this faith community and, perhaps, a binding force within the church as such.

Why should we have been so taken with this? There is more about the suffering of the church in the New Testament than about any other single aspect of the doctrine of the church. I had even written my doctoral thesis for Union Theological Seminary on "The Suffering of the Church." And I remember hearing Reinhold Niebuhr, on more than one occasion, speaking of the seminary community itself as "this community of suffering and prayer." So what was new in the Crossroads situation?

What was new, I think, was the *recognition* of this mark of the church within this remarkable congregation. "Church" as it is all-too-commonly practiced in North American middle-class Protestantism is frequently an exercise in repression. We may talk about the suffering of Jesus or of exceptional persons in Christian history (Dietrich Bonhoeffer, Martin Luther King, Oscar Romero), but most of us try to bear our crosses alone. It's unseemly, embarrassing, maudlin to express pain publicly, even to a few others, maybe even to one's pastor! Who wants tears at the coffee-hour? How socially unnerved most of us are by the mere mention of the term "cancer"! When even ordinary things like family tension or financial loss or high-school failure have to be kept "in the family," how can Christian congregations be expected to deal with job loss or divorce or sexual scandal? I won't even mention AIDS!

I certainly don't want to suggest that, at Crossroads, decorum is thrown to the winds! People don't go around talking about themselves and their problems and pains, or listening for confessions of suffering from others! The point is not the sharing of personal suffering but the fact that it *can* be shared. It doesn't have to be kept to oneself, bottled up, where it can destroy one. Members of this congregation know that they can speak, not only with their pastor, but with one another about their deepest concerns and fears, as about their hopes and joys. Church membership here is not based on bourgeois niceness but on truth and compassion, the gifts of grace made active in faith.

Last year, my wife and I became associate members of the Church of the Crossroads. We wanted to be participants in this fascinating community of Christ's discipleship. Just prior to the ceremony of our reception, a thoughtful member of the church semi-seriously remarked to me in passing that I may be *too* positive about Crossroads. "Crossroads isn't perfect!" he warned. Of course it isn't! The idea of a perfect church is an oxymoron! In fact, the essence of the church, in classical Protestant tradition, has to do with the fact that it confesses its sin!

But (as I said to the congregation on this occasion) for me, Crossroads exemplifies something far better than perfection (whatever that would mean!). It exemplifies Christian *authenticity*. In the shorthand lingo of the sixties, it's "for real." And anyone like me who feels that the besetting sin of North American mainline Protestantism has been its "unreality"—its tendency to play at religion—would know what an amazing thing it is to find, at last, a church that's "for real." There are a lot of us out there, I would still suggest (as I did in one of my first books[1]) who feel that while the Christian message has a lot to say to contemporary humankind, the Christian churches have pursued forms of religion and worship which do more to conceal that message than to communicate it. We are waiting to find out whether anything good can still come out of Nazareth—whether the church can reflect a little more clearly the reality of its Lord.

---

1. Hall, *The Reality of the Gospel and the Unreality of the Churches.*

Foreword

One day Rhoda and I were having lunch in the huge food court of the Ala Moana Center shopping complex. In that noisy marketplace of the post-modern world, redolent of multiculturalism, religious plurality, secularity, and every other wondrous and problematic dimension of our threatened planet, we found ourselves at a table next to a couple somewhat younger than ourselves. A conversation began with the usual where-are-you-from-ism but it soon moved to more interesting revelations. The woman of the pair told us that she was an active Roman Catholic and had lived in Honolulu most of her life. When I told her that I was there to be theologian-in-residence in one of the churches, she piped up immediately, "Crossroads?"

The point is, it's not only in the church that "reality" makes a difference! A church that is as real as this one, in today's consumer society, makes a difference in its worldly context too. Crossroads is not a big church—nothing of the vaunted megachurch about it (*Deo gratia!*). The church does not have to be big to be noticed, it only has to be true, just, engaged—real! Jesus, as someone wisely said, did not say "Count my sheep"; he said "Feed my sheep." I have been fed by this community of suffering and prayer, and so have many others, both within and beyond Crossroads itself.

Preface

THIS BOOK HAS BEEN inspired by the members of the church of which I am pastor and also by the theological work of Douglas John Hall, Professor Emeritus of Christian Theology at McGill University who, in his writing and teaching for over forty years, has sought to explore the various dimensions of Christian theology in a North American context. Two central themes run through Hall's theology: 1) a recognition that Christendom, as we have known it for the past fifteen centuries, is being disestablished among the formerly established churches of North America; and 2) a theology of the cross (*theologia crucis*), in contrast to the theology of glory (*theologia gloriae*) which has dominated the theology of Christendom, has the capacity to speak to these same churches in a way that may assist them to make their way faithfully through this time of transition in their life, ministry, and mission.

For six weeks in January and February of 2003, Dr. Hall served as a theologian-in-residence at Church of the Crossroads in Honolulu, Hawai'i, the United Church of Christ congregation of which I am pastor. His wife, Rhoda Hall, a creative and gifted person in her own right, accompanied him. While at the church, Dr. Hall led a study on his book *Why Christian?*, gave two sermons, presented a series of public lectures on his journey as a Christian theologian, and conducted a number of additional adult education classes. Church of the Crossroads had invited him to spend time with the congregation because some members had heard him speak on a previous visit to Hawai'i, and because throughout the years of my ministry in the United Church of Christ, I had been an avid reader of his many books in which he develops his contextual theology and explores a possible future for Christian faith in a post-Christendom world.

His time with us at Church of the Crossroads bore fruit in at least two ways. First, he gave the members of the church a vocabulary that enabled them to articulate more clearly their Christian faith in the context of their lived experience in the world. Secondly, he also helped the congregation to further clarify its identity and mission within the context of the culture and the religiously pluralistic world which surrounds it. At the close of his time with us, he suggested that I spend some time away to write about the congregation, feeling that the way in which Church of the Crossroads is responding to the new reality it now faces is a story that ought to be told.

Church of the Crossroads recognizes that the liberal Protestant Christianity which at one time dominated American culture is undergoing great change and the churches that represented it in the past no longer hold a position of power and influence in today's society. Church of the Crossroads has also observed that many mainline churches are looking for ways to become successful once again. Many such ventures focus on bringing more members into the church by popularizing the Gospel through utilizing new technologies and uncritically embracing American cultural values that revolve around personal happiness and security and a life devoid of suffering. These same attempts by the churches to be successful, however, often end up negating the overriding experience of hopelessness and despair to be found in so many people today.

Church of the Crossroads believes that new ways to both honor and communicate the truth of the Gospel in the context of human life as it is really lived and experienced in today's world must be found. In seeking to do this, the congregation feels that it is on the edge of the new and is eager to move into uncharted waters. This book describes the themes, struggles, and opportunities which emerge when congregations like Church of the Crossroads seek to embrace the awkwardness of their present existence as they journey towards a more faithful future.

The writing of the book was made possible through a generous Clergy Renewal Grant awarded to Church of the Crossroads by the Lilly Endowment. The grant gave me the opportunity to spend the last half of the year 2004 in Montréal, Canada, where I was able to converse extensively with Douglas and Rhoda Hall while I was working on the manuscript. In Montréal, I experienced firsthand a Christendom which has been disestablished. Both the Catholic and Protestant churches of this vibrant and interesting city have lost their former position of power and influence and are, for the most part, struggling to keep their doors open. I am told that in this city, there are at least forty Catholic properties up for sale! Although there are signs of renewal here and there, for the most part, Montréal churches seem to carry on their life and ministry as though they were still at the center of the culture rather than on the periphery. The

Preface

situation faced by the mainline Protestant churches in Hawai'i may not be as dire, but one cannot help but notice that they too occupy a much less prominent place in the society than they once did.

In this book, I seek to address this new situation. In a way, this book is about Church of the Crossroads, its history, its engagement with the world, the pastoral dimensions of its life as a community, the ways in which it gathers for worship, and its ethos as a congregation. Yet, in my writing, I have had a larger context in mind. I am writing this book not only to describe Church of the Crossroads but also to place it in the context of the ongoing process of Christendom's disestablishment. I am also writing this book as an encouragement to other congregations, churches *at a crossroads*, who are ready to envision a new way of being in this time of transition.

I am grateful to the Lilly Foundation for making the writing of this book possible. I am also grateful to Douglas and Rhoda Hall for their friendship, counsel, and encouragement. I wish to thank Donna Stewart who read the manuscript carefully and offered helpful suggestions for improvement. I am grateful also for the love and support of my wife Leilani who was willing for us to live apart, except for two short times during the six months I was away from home.

Most of all, I am grateful to the good people of Church of the Crossroads. In a very real sense, this is their book. Not only were they my most basic "resource" in the writing, but throughout the last nineteen years, they have inspired and encouraged me to be the very best pastor and teacher I can be. To have been their pastor has been the greatest privilege of my life.

1

The Church in Context

Most of the world is now following a kind of right-wing fundamentalism. That is true in the South of the United States, and not only in the South, but it is also true, it seems, for Africa and Latin America, and, as far as Protestantism is concerned, also in Asia. In the Philippines, mainly Catholic, it is Opus Dei who brings the fundamentalist message; it is particularly active in Manila. This for me is kind of frightening, that this is the only evangelism we have. What do we have to offer in terms of evangelism?

—Renate Rose

It's the end of Christendom as we have known it. Today's world is a world of religious pluralism and diversity where major religions find it necessary to encounter the truth of other faiths, and this raises a whole new question. What is it that salvation means in universal terms? What does salvation really mean in a world of pluralism? And a final comment is that churches as institutions are no longer vehicles for the gospel they profess to embrace. In place of religion and churches as institutions, there is a movement embodied in "Christian entities" or "Christian communities." These manifest themselves not as much as institutions but as processes moving hopefully toward transformation.

—Mitsuo Aoki

I believe we are really seeing a new kind of Christendom. Political leaders are leaning on religion and using it for what they want, and so I think that although we are finding ourselves in the midst of a post-fourth-century Christendom, the effort to create a new Christendom is alive and well.

—Judy Rantala

The preceding are comments from members participating in adult education classes at Church of the Crossroads, June 2004. Additional comments from the same classes as well as other reflections from members of Church of the Crossroads will be found at the beginning of each subsequent chapter.

> *He called the crowd with his disciples, and said to them, "If any want to become my followers, let them deny themselves and take up their cross and follow me. For those who want to save their life will lose it and those who lose their life for my sake, and for the sake of the gospel, will save it. For what will it profit them to gain the whole world and forfeit their life?"* (Mark 8:34–36)

A REMARKABLE EVENT

I WILL BEGIN THIS book by describing a remarkable event in my life, and by implication, in the life of Church of the Crossroads. On a Sunday morning in August 2005, I was asked to address the John A. Burns Grassroots Democracy Luncheon, an annual gathering of the Democratic Party in Hawai'i. John A. Burns served as Hawai'i's first governor, from 1962 to 1974. The fact that the event took place at 10:30 on a Sunday morning speaks volumes. It was a clear indication that our society is, for the most part, a secular society. In years past, it would have been unheard of to schedule a public gathering on a Sunday morning. The title of my address was "The Intersection of Religion and Politics: Rediscovering the Common Good." I began my address with these words:

> It is an honor for me to have been asked to be here today and to share my thoughts on the way religion and politics might intersect in our time. The honor is not mine alone, but belongs even more so to the congregation I have served for the past seventeen years. Church of the Crossroads is a community of faith that throughout its eighty-two-year history has often acted out a deep commitment to justice and peace in our world, and on behalf of those who have been left out of the political process and those whose lives have been marked by poverty and powerlessness.

I went on to say that in my thirty-three years in the ordained ministry, I had never been asked to do anything like this. I noted that clergy who represent the churches of mainline Protestantism are rarely asked to speak to anyone other than the members of the congregations they serve or perhaps other religious groups. Occasionally, they are asked to give a blessing at a public gathering. Furthermore, clergy who are willing to speak out on issues of peace and justice have found themselves out of favor with many who currently hold political power in our society.

I continued:

> Political leaders find it more to their advantage these days to pay attention to those who belong to the Christian Right rather than people like me. Indeed, the Christian Right has succeeded not only in commanding the attention of political leaders but has also succeeded in shaping the moral values agenda that had such a tremendous influence on the outcome of the 2004 Presidential Election and which continues to define, unfortunately, I believe, the intersection of religion and politics in our time.

I assured the audience that I was not complaining, however, and continued,

> It's not a terrible thing to be out of favor. Being on the periphery of religious and cultural life gives one a tremendous freedom to articulate a larger moral vision than the narrow moral agenda that is in vogue these days.

In the course of the speech itself, I reintroduced the old democratic idea of the common good, which, when taken seriously, transcends special interest and goes beyond a narrow conception of what constitutes moral values. Governor Burns himself exemplified decision making based upon this principle of the common good when he, a good and devout Roman Catholic, allowed a bill to pass that overturned the abortion law in Hawai'i, thereby guaranteeing a woman's right to choose. Hawai'i was the first state in the union to do this, and it did so a number of years before Roe vs. Wade was heard by the Supreme Court of the United States.

In articulating a vision of the common good, I spoke out of my own Judeo-Christian heritage and said that this tradition points to God's concern for the whole of the human community, especially the poor, the hungry, and the destitute, and also for the well-being of the creation itself. I quoted from the psalms, the prophets, and Jesus. I then invited the members of the audience to explore their own religious and humanist traditions in order to explore their own vision of the common good.

At the close of the speech, I summarized my main points:

1. Our society is a religiously pluralistic society and largely a secular society. No one religious viewpoint should be allowed to shape public discourse and policy.

2. Christians who are currently out of favor ought to, on the basis of scriptural evidence, challenge openly and boldly those Christians who are controlled by a right wing ideology and a narrow conception of what constitutes moral values.

3. These same Christians ought to set themselves about the task of discerning what God wills for the common good of all, relying on those parts of the scriptural heritage that point to God's concern for all people, and the emphasis of the prophets and Jesus on distributive justice and the need to care for the neighbor, defined as every man, woman, and child who shares the common life of our society and world.

4. Those in political life ought to engage themselves in their own discernment of the common good, and then be willing to enter into dialogue with all who approach the question from their own religious, ethical, or humanist traditions.

5. We must not be silent and allow ideology, either political or religious, to dominate and control our political life and our public discourse surrounding moral values.

6. We must all seek to act out of a disinterest that enables us to move beyond our own self-interest and our own beliefs in order to consider that which will be good for all.

7. We must always understand that the government is the only thing we own in common. We are the government. Government belongs not to a religious group or to those who hold political power or to those who hold economic power in our society. It belongs to everyone, and everyone must have a voice in shaping a society that benefits all.

8. Finally, religious and political leaders must always be open to one another and respectful of one another as together they seek the common good of all.

The Church in Context

A CHURCH ON THE PERIPHERY

I must say that I was somewhat anxious about giving this speech. Would people understand what I was trying to say? Would the response be affirmative or negative? Well, about a dozen of the three hundred people who were present did walk out as I was speaking about a woman's right to choose. Some ran after them, urging them to remain for the rest of the speech, but they continued to head toward the elevators. Those who remained enthusiastically affirmed what I had to say.

Since then, the speech has been disseminated far and wide through the Internet. Groups on the islands other than Oʻahu have gathered to read and discuss it. I must say that the response has amazed me. I have come to realize that churches like Church of the Crossroads can indeed engage the world, and that there are many people who want the mainline Protestant churches to address issues of peace and social justice openly with passion and conviction. These same people, most of whom would never enter the doors of a church, are looking for a language they can use to address those on the right who have dominated the discourse around moral values.

When I spoke that Sunday morning, it was really Church of the Crossroads speaking. Every member of this two-hundred-person congregation agreed with the main ideas of the speech. They were aware of the event before it took place and were anxious to hear how everything went. Unlike so many pastors who engage in public witness, I felt that when I spoke that Sunday morning, I was really representing the congregation I serve. My speech, then, was both an individual and a corporate expression. Since the event, I have come to appreciate that throughout the eighty-four years of its existence, this congregation has been intentional in enabling its members to engage in theological education and reflection. I believe that the members of a congregation do not arrive at this kind of shared understanding by accident. It takes intentionality. It takes years of devoted study, discussion, and discernment by everyone involved.

In giving the speech, I also sensed a tremendous freedom to speak openly and honestly to a gathering of people that included a number of elected officials. Often, the church has not enjoyed this kind of freedom. The church has been so linked to the centers of political and social power that it has been less than free to speak truth to power.

Church of the Crossroads has never occupied a position of prestige and power in the political and social life of Hawaiʻi. In recent years, it has found itself even more so on the periphery. Being on the periphery brings a measure of uncertainty. The old assumptions about what it means to be a "church" no longer suffice. Everything becomes fluid and tentative. At the same time, being on the periphery of social and political life brings new possibilities. When a church is set free from the constraints that in the past resulted from a grasping for position, power, and prestige, it is able to get in touch with the original spirit and message of the Gospel, which has always been, when honestly proclaimed, bold, new, and unconventional.

THE THEME OF THIS BOOK

In this book, I will draw upon the life and experience of Church of the Crossroads in order to describe both the uncertainties and possibilities that exist when a church not only recognizes but also affirms its changing status in the world. I trust that what I write will provide a measure of encouragement to mainline Protestant churches, which are presently experiencing an uncertain existence in the North American context and are consequently seeking to be "church" in a new and faithful way.

In a very real sense, these churches exist between a Constantinian Christianity and a Christianity that is to be. I believe that the uncertainty the mainline Protestant churches are facing is due to the fact that they are being disestablished from their former position of power and influence within the larger society. The process of disestablishment they are undergoing is a consequence of the broader disestablishment of Christendom, which was initiated by the Emperor Constantine and has dominated the Western church for nearly sixteen centuries.

In facing the uncertainty of their present life and ministry, the churches of mainline Protestantism are, for the most part, responding in one of two ways. Some are simply choosing to ignore the process of their disestablishment. They continue to carry on with their church life as though nothing were happening, as though they were still occupying a place at the center of society.

Others, knowing that they are being moved to the periphery of social and political life, are seeking to regain their past power and influence by adopting one or another program of church growth. Usually, these church growth schemes originate in the newly emerging megachurches of the Christian right. By adopting one of these programs for church growth, the formerly established churches of mainline Protestantism are hoping they will once again find themselves in a position of power and influence in the larger society. They hope they will once again be "successful" churches, which, in terms of American cultural values, means that they will enjoy large memberships and command the attention of the media and those who occupy the seats of power in the society. In choosing the success-driven path of the megachurches, however, these churches must leave behind and abandon much of what has been worthwhile and faithful in the mainline Protestant tradition, including the openness with which Protestantism has at times entertained minority theological points-of-view and the faithful witness of many Protestant Christians and churches as they have sought to address issues of peace and justice in our world over the years.

In this book, I propose an alternative to the two options described above: both the option of ignoring the process of disestablishment that is taking place, and the option that seeks to regain the kind of power and influence in the larger society that once was but is no longer enjoyed. I am suggesting a third option. *I am suggesting that the churches of mainline Protestantism embrace their ongoing disestablishment and see their disestablishment not as a burden or as something to be either ignored or reversed, but as an opportunity to envision a new way of being in the world.* Inasmuch as they are able to do this with a measure of authenticity and intentionality, they will be strengthened to make their way towards a more faithful future. I will further suggest that a new way of being in the world will become possible only as the churches of mainline Protestantism replace the theology of glory (*theologia gloriae*) that has dominated the life of established Christianity throughout the centuries with a theology of the cross (*theologia crucis*), which has served as a minority theological tradition at various times in the history of the Christian church.

Throughout this book, I will draw upon the life and experience of Church of the Crossroads, a member church of the United Church of Christ in Honolulu, Hawai'i. As I noted in the speech I gave at the John A. Burns Democracy Lunch, I have been privileged to serve this congregation as its pastor and teacher for many years, now approaching twenty. Church of the Crossroads is a smaller church with a membership of just over two hundred people. Its membership is remarkably diverse in terms of ethnic and racial backgrounds, age, sexual orientation, economic standing, and theological perspective. It is a congregation that has always been concerned about the needs of the world. With its buildings located next to the University of Hawai'i at Mānoa Campus, it has placed great value in an educated and articulate laity. It is a church where you don't have to "leave your mind at the doorstep before entering." Of course, not everyone is interested in becoming part of such a congregation. It would be a mistake to say that this congregation is able to include everyone. No church can do that. Yet, for all its limitations, it is a remarkable congregation, nonetheless. What makes it particularly remarkable is the way in which it has embraced its minority position within the larger society without becoming silent in the face of the world's injustices. It continues to be a church that is "in the world," but not "of the world." It is also a congregation that is consciously choosing to leave behind the theology of glory that has dominated the Western Church for centuries and is instead beginning to take seriously a theology of the cross.

Even as I draw upon the life and experience of this particular congregation in my writing, I will have in mind a larger context: namely, churches like Church of the Crossroads that are faced with the task of "being church" in a time of their ongoing disestablishment. Hence, I have chosen *Church at a Crossroads* as the title for this book.

A CHURCH OF A DIASPORA

One way to describe Church of the Crossroads is to say that it is a church that sees itself as belonging to a diaspora—a scattering or dispersal. It not only recognizes, but also accepts its diaspora status in the world. "Diaspora" is the word the Roman Catholic theologian Karl Rahner uses to describe the nature of the present-day Christian Church. He says that every Christian church really belongs to a diaspora. The Christian churches have been scattered throughout the world. "My thesis," he writes,

> is this. Insofar as our outlook is really based on today, and looking towards tomorrow, the present situation of Christians can be characterized as that of a *diaspora*: and this signifies, in terms of the history of salvation, a "must," from which we may and must draw conclusions about our behavior as Christians.[1]

Rahner, in supporting this notion, goes on to say that Christianity exists everywhere in the world and everywhere as a diaspora. There are no

---

1. Rahner, *Mission and Grace: Essays on Pastoral Theology*, vol. 1, 20.

longer any Christian countries. Christianity "is, effectually, *in terms of numbers*, a minority everywhere."[2]

This is how Church of the Crossroads understands itself. Accepting its diaspora status, it has shaped for itself an identity as a Christian community "on the edge," honoring the parts of its history that speak of struggle and change, creatively engaging the world, affirming the stories of its members that bear the marks of both suffering and hope, gathering for worship in ways that are authentic and renewing, and reflecting a particular ethos, or spirit, around which it carries out its life, ministry, and witness.

As a church of a diaspora, Church of the Crossroads sees itself against the backdrop of Christendom's establishment in the West initiated by the Emperor Constantine in the fourth century CE and its subsequent disestablishment, a process that can be traced as far back as the thirteenth century. These are the two defining events that have shaped not only Church of the Crossroads but also the present life of the Christian Church as a whole.

I will describe these two defining events in greater detail. I will also relate Christendom's establishment to the ascendancy of the theology of glory, which became the predominant theology of the church after the fourth century, and the potential efficacy of a theology of the cross for churches that are now experiencing their diaspora status, their own disestablishment within the broader context of Western Christendom's disestablishment.

THE ESTABLISHMENT OF CHRISTENDOM

In the post-Biblical world, the first defining event in the life of the Christian Church was the establishment of Christianity as the official religion of the West in the fourth century CE. Prior to this time, the Christian movement had struggled to keep itself alive as one religious option among many. It received no endorsement from any political entity, for its message arising out of its commitment to the reign of God was construed as being in conflict with, if not opposition to, any political establishment. Moreover, within its own life, there existed all kinds of beliefs and forms of spirituality, making its continuation as a movement uncertain indeed.

---

2. Ibid., 25.

As Douglas John Hall states, the only thing that kept it alive was its confession of faith.

> What nurtured and sustained the church from Pentecost to the second decade of the fourth century was not an automatic and predictable translation of each new cohort of human beings into the Christian fold, but rather the decisions of individual persons to believe and follow the One whom they heard Christians confessing. In the pre-Constantinian situation, confessing the faith was an aspect of every Christian life.[3]

The emperor Constantine began to change all that. He inherited a Roman empire that itself needed to be united, and he saw the Christian religion as the tool for solidifying his empire. And so, Constantine adopted Christianity as his unifying principle. Yet, for Christianity to be an effective tool for unification, it too needed to be unified. For this reason, Constantine called together the Council of Nicaea in 325 CE, and a unity of belief and doctrine within the church was achieved.

The establishment of Christianity as the religion of the Roman Empire, begun by Constantine, was completed by the time of Theodosius the Great, who ruled as emperor at the close of the fourth century CE. The transformation of the Christian faith into an organized religion was remarkable. At the beginning of the fourth century, it is estimated that Christians comprised no more than one-tenth of the population of the empire. In the span of just seventy or eighty years, to be a member of the empire was virtually to be a member of the church! Anyone who did not adhere to the faith and doctrine of the church was not to be tolerated. The Code of Theodosius, formulated in the year 380 CE, tells the story.

> It is our desire that all the various nations which are subject to our Clemency and Moderation, should continue in the profession of that religion which was delivered to the Romans by the divine Apostle Peter, as it hath been preserved by faithful tradition; and which is now professed by the Pontiff Damasus and by Peter, Bishop of Alexandria, a man of apostolic holiness. According to the apostolic teaching and the doctrine of the Gospel, let us believe the one deity of the Father, the Son and the Holy Spirit, in equal majesty and in a holy Trinity. We authorize the followers of this law to assume the title of Catholic Christians; but as for the others, since, in our judgement, they are foolish madmen, we

---

3. Hall, *Confessing the Faith*, 6.

decree that they shall be branded by the ignominious name of heretics, and shall not presume to give to their conventicles the name of churches. They will suffer in the first place the chastisement of divine condemnation, and in the second the punishment which our authority, in accordance with the will of Heaven, shall decide to inflict.[4]

Loren B. Mead has described the consequences of Christendom's establishment this way:

> In Christendom there could be only one church within one political entity. To be *outside* that unity was unthinkable, impossible. To be outside the faith was to be outside the community. Heresy and treason were two sides of the same thing. In such a paradigm people who were disloyal to the faith or to the nation could be tortured, oppressed, or killed precisely because they were profoundly "other"; to be fully a human being was to be a Christian and a member of the Empire.[5]

I hope you will agree with me that Jesus surely never intended his followers to organize themselves into anything remotely resembling Constantine's enterprise! I hope you will also entertain the thought that Christendom has been a curse as much as it has been a blessing. On the one hand, it has produced art of great beauty, architectural wonders, and yes, music. What would our lives be without the music of Bach and Mozart? Yet, on the other hand, it has fostered violence against its opponents, the devaluation of women and people of color, untold oppression against all who would question its authority, an anti-Semitism that led to the Holocaust, and the denigration of other world religions as well as indigenous religions. It has aligned itself with political authority to the detriment of minority peoples. It has obscured the biblical truth that the sovereignty of God, a sovereignty based in the power of suffering and love rather than in the power of might, is to be honored above all other sovereignties, whether that of nation or empire. It has distorted the life of Jesus, who preferred the company of the outcast and sinner to those who were in power, and who was reported to have said: "Render to Caesar the things that are Caesar's and to God the things that are God's" (Mark 12:17).

---

4. Bettenson, *Documents of the Christian Church*, 2nd ed. 22.
5. Mead, *The Once and Future Church*, 16.

THE THEOLOGY OF GLORY AND THE THEOLOGY OF THE CROSS

As Constantinian Christianity became the established religion of the West, it lost sight of the original spirit of the Christian movement. In its rise, the human Jesus of the gospels was neglected in favor of the Christ of glory. One could argue that the Nicaean Creed (325 CE) and later the Formula of Chalcedon (451 CE), using Greek categories of substance, affirmed the full humanity of Jesus. In reality, however, the human Jesus was set aside and neglected. The Christ of glory suited a glorious empire better. And, as Douglas John Hall argues, the Formula of Chalcedon, that Jesus Christ is at once "complete in Godhead and complete in manhood . . . of one substance with the Father as regards his Godhead, and at the same time of one substance with us as regards his manhood"[6] did not in the end deliver a Jesus who experienced the existential despair so many of us experience. It did not deliver Christianity from a "theoretical incarnationalism lacking in existential depth and human credibility."[7]

In actuality, the Christ of glory took precedence over the human Jesus who was born in a feeding trough for animals (which we sentimentally refer to as a manger), who welcomed the poor and the sinner to his table, who pronounced judgment on the rich and the religious and who wandered about the countryside delivering good news to the oppressed, who ran into trouble with both the Jewish temple elite and the Roman authorities, and who was put to death by the Roman empire. How ironic, and also how strange, that this Jesus became the religious hero of that same empire!

Constantinian Christianity, simply because it was a religion of the empire, could not help but adhere to a theology of glory (*theologia gloriae*) with its focus on the glorified, resurrected Christ, and therefore was incapable of entertaining a theology of the cross (*theologia crucis*) with its focus on the human Jesus. The newly established Christian Church, now the handmaid of a powerful and often oppressive empire, could not afford to concentrate too much on the reality of suffering that lies at the center of the humanity of Jesus and *is* the reality of the cross. Instead, the cross was used by the empire as an agent of power and conquest. For the newly established church, power and authority were far more important

---

6. Bettenson, *Documents of the Christian Church*, 73.
7. Hall, *Professing the Faith*, 400.

goals than solidarity with the suffering of the world. This neglect of a theology of the cross and its accompanying acknowledgment of the reality of human suffering has persisted in the church, with a few exceptions, until the present day.

As a theological perspective, the theology of the cross (*theologia crucis*) was first named by the theologian Martin Luther in the sixteenth century. However, he did not invent it. The theology of the cross can be traced back through some of the medieval mystics to Paul and even back to the prophetic tradition of ancient Israel. Martin Luther, in giving a name to this particular theological perspective, contrasted it to the theology of glory, which had dominated Constantinian Christianity.

Luther contrasted the two theologies in the presentation he gave in April, 1518, at his monastic order's chapter meeting when he was called to give an account of himself following the wide circulation of his Ninety-Five Theses. Two sentences in this regard are noteworthy:

> (20) He deserves to be called a theologian, however, who comprehends the visible and manifest things of God seen through suffering and the cross.
>
> (21) A theology of glory [*theologia gloriae*] calls evil good and good evil. A theology of the cross [*theologia crucis*] calls the thing what it actually is.[8]

One way to understand what Luther meant by a theology of glory is to link it to the term *triumphalism*. As a religious perspective on the world and human experience, triumphalism focuses on God's power and majesty and ends up setting aside any serious consideration of God's compassion and suffering. It emphasizes solutions and answers to life's problems and devalues the ambiguities, the uncertainties, the questions and doubts that are part and parcel of human existence. Its brilliance and certitude accentuate the positive and overlook the negative. It posits a suffering-free existence and fails to account for the reality of human suffering.

The theology of glory, with its attendant triumphalism, has functioned through the centuries as a religious ideology. We can define ideology as "a theoretical statement or system of interpretation that functions for its adherents as a full and sufficient credo, a source of personal authority, and an intellectually and psychologically comforting insulation from

---

8. See Lull, *Martin Luther's Basic Theological Writings*, 30 ff.

the frightening and chaotic mishmash of daily existence."[9] When the ideological nature of the theology of glory is understood, one can appreciate its attractiveness as a theological position. By inviting people to buy into a religious ideology that resolves everything, answers all questions, and dispels all doubts, the theology of glory allows middle-class Christians and churches to gloss over, ignore, and repress the underlying experience of meaninglessness and despair that, for the most part, characterizes the suffering of those who live in our affluent society. The problem is that, as in the case of all ideologies, whether religious or political, the triumphalism at the center of the theology of glory ends up distorting reality by ignoring the negative aspects of human experience. In Luther's words, it "calls good evil and evil good." In the end, it cannot help but be unsatisfactory, for it fails to acknowledge the reality of human suffering and is therefore incapable of speaking to the totality of our human experience.

Only a theology of the cross can do that. As Luther stated, the theology of the cross "calls the thing what it actually is." Human suffering is just what it is. It is not an illusion. The theology of the cross is able to call human suffering what it actually is because, as a reality, it is *encompassed in God's own being*. In the theology of the cross, God is understood as One whose power is defined primarily by a compassion that embraces the suffering of humankind. This divine compassion, which we find at the center of the theology of the cross, is in marked contrast to the all-controlling power that defines the character of God in the theology of glory. If God is in complete control over creation, then God must be responsible for all human suffering. In the theology of glory, this reality of suffering to which we are all subject is explained away rather than addressed. On the other hand, if the nature of God is characterized primarily by compassion, literally *with-suffering*, then God becomes fully present in the suffering of human beings. God gives up God's own control over the created order in choosing to suffer with humankind and indeed with the whole of creation.

For the Christian, the compassion of God, the desire of God to suffer with those who suffer, is revealed most especially in the cross of Jesus. In contemplating the cross of Jesus, the human being is led to both acknowledge the suffering that is part of his or her human experience and also come to experience the hope that can arise in the midst of that suffering.

---

9. Hall, *The Cross in Our Context*, 25.

For if God is present in the cross, and therefore involved in the suffering that Jesus must undergo, we human beings can then find hope in our own suffering, simply because it is God who suffers with us.

In choosing to suffer with humankind, the intention of God is not that human beings should continue to suffer, but that they might be brought to life and wholeness. In this sense, a theology of the cross by no means rules out the glory of God. Irenaeus once said that "the glory of God is humankind [being made] fully alive." This idea of glory is, however, very different than the glory associated with the *theology* of glory. That theology attributes glory as belonging exclusively to the godhead itself. In the theology of the cross, on the other hand, God does not seek glory for God's own self; God, rather, seeks to glorify the creature. God's glory is the human being who is fully alive and whole and authentic.

A THEOLOGY NOT WELL LOVED

The theology of the cross has become important for Church of the Crossroads. However, it has taken considerable study and reflection by the members of the congregation in order to arrive at an appreciation of this theology. Inasmuch as the cross is so central a symbol in the Gospels themselves, one would think that a theology of the cross would occupy a central place in the theology of the church. Yet, it has functioned as a "thin" tradition in the church. Jürgen Moltmann has written, "There is a good deal of support in the tradition for the theology of the cross, but it was never much loved."[10] Why it has not been much loved as a tradition may be understood once we realize how triumphalism, as a religious ideology, has dominated Christian theology for a very long time. A triumphal religion that has been so encompassing is almost incapable of entertaining any idea or notion that would cause it to question its own assumptions. For this reason, the theology of the cross has never received much consideration by mainstream Christianity in the West. This may well explain why the theology of the cross has not been easily appropriated by Church of the Crossroads, or any church, for that matter.

Other factors have also contributed to the neglect of this theology. Luther's distinction between the theology of glory and the theology of the cross was often lost or set aside as Protestantism established itself in the northern nations of Europe and then on the North American continent.

10. Moltmann, *The Crucified God*, 3.

The newly emerging Protestantism following the Reformation soon sought to align itself with political power and authority of one kind or another, and in doing so, it returned to a theology of glory that would better suit its desire to be established legally and/or culturally. And consequently, the theology of the cross with its theme of suffering has continued to exist only as a thin tradition in the Christian church. It has always so existed on the fringe of the North American church. Writes Hall,

> In the North American context, this transmutation, neglect, and distortion of the theme of Christian suffering has been especially conspicuous, for, in addition to the usual ecclesiastical preference for a theology and ecclesiology "of glory," Christianity on this continent has been compounded with modernity's insistence upon progress, "happiness" and the elimination of all pain.[11]

Rather than take up a theology of the cross and its accompanying focus on the reality of human suffering, established Protestantism moved along with its easy relationship to social and political power, and in the North American context, with its blessing of the cultural value of success, the belief in unending progress, the spirit of optimism, and a suffering-free life. The spiritual core of the Reformation found in Luther's theology of the cross, with some exceptions, has not yet found its way into the life of the church. However, it is still there, waiting to be appropriated. Douglas John Hall writes,

> If this spiritual core of the Reformation was seldom applied to Protestant relations with powerful governments and classes—if it remained dormant at the ethical level and hardly even entertained theologically—it was nonetheless there at the center, waiting to assert itself and, here and there, be grasped with conviction and imagination. The assumptions and allures of establishment have been such, however, that apart from individual and small group claims upon this "thin tradition," Protestantism has preferred to limp through most of its history following two paths, ultimately divergent: the path of political quietism or noninterference, and that of personal piety. The cross could sometimes be a meaningful symbol for the latter, but not for the former.[12]

The deeper meaning of the theology of the cross, that the death of Jesus reveals God's abiding commitment to the world and God's own soli-

---

11. Hall, *Confessing the Faith*, 96.
12. Ibid., 209.

darity with all who suffer, could not be completely ignored once it had been introduced into the world of theological discourse. This theology stands against every temptation to abandon creation and seek security in an individualistic faith that ignores the needs of the world and answers too easily and quickly the problem of human suffering.

There have been minority and/or significant voices within established Christianity that have professed this *theologia crucis* from time to time. They include Dietrich Bonhoeffer and the Confessing Church movement in Germany, and also Reinhold Niebuhr, Paul Tillich, and Dorothee Soëlle. However, the theology of the cross has remained largely dormant, waiting for the time when it might emerge once again in the life of the church. That time may be now.

CHRISTENDOM'S DISESTABLISHMENT

To summarize, the establishment of Christianity as the religion of the West was the first defining event in the history of the Christian church. In its desire to achieve a position of power and prominence in the world, Christendom embraced a theology of glory that overshadowed any consideration of a theology of the cross. It reigned supreme for at least thirteen centuries, and its spirit and legacy are still with us.

We turn now to the second defining event in the history of the Christian church, and that is Christendom's disestablishment, which is no less momentous than its establishment. It is a process that has been going on for some time and it is a process that will continue for a long time into the future. After all, when one realizes that Christianity has existed at the center of Western culture for centuries, it is no small matter for Christianity to be disestablished as the religion of the West.

The vestiges of Constantinian Christendom will be around for a long time in the churches of the West, both in the Roman Catholic Church and in the churches of mainline Protestantism. At Church of the Crossroads, we sometimes speak and act as though our congregation occupied a position of far greater power and importance in the society than it actually does. In other words, we often give the impression of being an establishment church. We are coming to realize, however, that we are in fact being disestablished. This is also true with all of the once-established churches of North America. The ongoing disestablishment of Western Christendom is evidenced not only in the numerical loss of their members, but also, and perhaps more significantly, in the loss of their cultural and political influence.

The question surely arises: What has accounted for this second defining event in the history of the Christian church, this ongoing process of disestablishment? Douglas Hall has written extensively about the root causes of this phenomenon.[13] In summary, he has said that the dissolution of Western Christendom began when faith was separated from reason. Beginning in the thirteenth century, the synthesis between faith and reason that had dominated Christian theology began to break down under the impact of the new Aristotelian rationality. Thomas Aquinas attempted to save the synthesis by separating faith and reason and by positing them as two separable sources of truth. It was inevitable that the synthesis would be in trouble once thinkers began to employ reason and empirical data in order to challenge religious truth. By the time of William of Ockham and the Nominalists of the late Middle Ages, a certain skepticism had crept into Christian theology. Reason was increasingly given an independent role and faith became less accessible to rational investigation. Matters of faith were subject to the authority of the church, but not matters of reason. Christian theology ended up abandoning reason as a source of truth, and as a consequence, the Christian church became increasingly incapable of incorporating into its life any kind of dialogue with doubt. Meanwhile, doubt based on reason continued to flourish and found its fullest expression in the Enlightenment of the eighteenth century.

Hall points out that the Protestant Reformation continued the movement towards the disestablishment of Christendom in two ways. First, the Reformation created a division in a Christendom that had depended upon the unity principle to keep it established. Secondly, the Reformation introduced a theology that, when it was taken seriously, could not abide with anything like an establishment, although it most often ended up seeking establishment, both legal and cultural, nonetheless.

It is a mistake, Hall maintains, to blame the demise of Christendom on secularism, multiculturalism, and religious pluralism. To lay the blame on these factors ignores the deeper causes of its demise. Secularism itself is a consequence of the separation of faith and reason. As reason claimed its own autonomous position in the intellectual landscape, it gave rise to the possibility of a secular life lived without recourse to Christian faith and

---

13. See Hall, *Confessing the Faith*, 204–11.

practice. In other words, secularism came about as Christianity ceased to appeal to reason to substantiate its claims. Secularism, then, can hardly be blamed for the depreciation of Christianity in contemporary society! Multiculturalism, secularism, and religious pluralism are simply realities in our modern world. Christian faith and Christian communities must now find their way in the midst of these realities.

DISESTABLISHMENT IN THE NORTH AMERICAN CONTEXT

All of this talk about disestablishment may seem a little strange to North American Christians. After all, in both Canada and the United States, we have what is known as the principle of the separation of church and state. That principle has meant that there has been no established state church in Canada or the United States, at least since the collapse of the Christian hegemonies that were attempted in the northern nations of the North American continent in the seventeenth century. In the Massachusetts Bay Colony, it was the Congregationalists who sought to establish themselves both socially and politically as the official church. Diana Eck, in her recent book, *A New Religious America*, writes:

> The Pilgrims who sailed the seas to establish communities in a new world wanted to be free to practice their religious faith. But they were not thinking about a wider ethic of religious freedom when they clung to the shores of the Atlantic and built the first cabins in what is now Plymouth. They were thinking about how to survive in the wilderness of a new world. As the decades brought more and more settlers to these shores, our Christian ancestors did not create widely tolerant communities. The Puritans of Boston envisioned a society, a biblical commonwealth, decisively shaped by their own form of Christianity. They were concerned primarily with religious freedom for themselves and did not regard it as a foundation for common life with people who differed from them.[14]

And so it was that in Puritan Boston, Solomon Franco, a Sephardic Jewish merchant, was "warned" out of town. Between 1659 and 1661, this same religious establishment put four Quakers to death on the gallows on Boston Common. Roger Williams and Anne Hutchinson had to flee from the Massachusetts Bay Colony because of their nonconformist religious beliefs. At his Massachusetts trial in 1635, Roger Williams declared,

---

14. Eck, *A New Religious America*, 36.

> I do affirm it to be against the testimony of Christ Jesus for the civil state to impose upon the soul of the people a religion, a worship, a ministry. The state should give free and absolute permission of conscience to all men in what is spiritual alone. Ye have lost yourselves! Your breath blows out the candle of liberty in this land.[15]

The same spirit of establishment that dominated the life of the Massachusetts Bay Colony was repeated elsewhere on the continent. In Virginia, it was the Church of England that, as in Upper Canada, sought to be the established church. In Maryland, it was the Protestants, and in New York, it was the Dutch Reformed Church. These hegemonies did not persist, however.

In her book, Diana Eck enumerates the important events that took place as the new nation moved towards the separation of church and state. First, the colony of Rhode Island had no established church and permitted religious freedom for everyone. It was to Rhode Island that Roger Williams fled. Then, the citizens of Flushing, in New Amsterdam (now the state of New York), in 1657 drew up the Flushing Remonstrance, which opposed a ruling by Peter Stuyvesant banning Quakers from the colony. As Eck points out, the Flushing Remonstrance was more about the principle of hospitality than it was about freedom of conscience. It remains an important document, nonetheless, on the road to the separation of church and state. Next, Eck draws our attention to William Penn who offered the Pennsylvania colony as a place of refuge for Quakers who had been persecuted in England and Ireland. Penn's invitation to the Quakers was based on his adherence to the notion of freedom of conscience.

In the colony of Virginia, the Church of England received the benefits of an established church. However, the Presbyterians of Hanover asked, "Why should Presbyterians be taxed to support the Anglican Church?" The statement of these Hanover Presbyterians argues against the establishment of *Christianity* as such and not just the establishment of *a Christian church*. The document declares that Christianity should not be established in America any more than Islam should be established as the official religion of the society.

> In this enlightened age, and in a land where all, of every denomination are united in the most strenuous efforts to be free, we hope and expect that our representatives will cheerfully concur in re-

---

15. Williams, citation from his trial, *Living With Our Deepest Differences*, 32.

moving every species of religious, as well as civil bondage. Certain it is, that every argument for civil liberty gains additional strength when applied to liberty in the concerns of religion, and there is no argument in favour of establishing the Christian religion, but what may be pleaded, with equal propriety, for establishing the tenets of Mahomed by those who believe the Alcoran: or if this be not true, it is at least impossible for the magistrate to adjudge the right of preference among the various sects that profess the Christian faith, without erecting a chair of infallibility, which would lead us back to the church of Rome.[16]

The battle to disestablish the Church of England in Virginia went on for ten years. Eventually, in 1777, Thomas Jefferson first drafted "An Act for the Establishment of Religious Freedom," arguing that the freedom of conscience is compromised by the establishment of any religion. Finally, in 1786, the Virginia Statute for Religious Freedom was passed, which in turn became a model for the principles of the separation of church and state and for the protection of religious freedom that were finally guaranteed in the Bill of Rights in 1791.

CHRISTENDOM IN THE STATE OF HAWAI'I

Since there are no state-established churches now in Canada or the United States, we might wonder about all this talk of Christendom and its collapse and ask whether this idea of Christendom has ever been really operative in North American life and culture, at least since 1791. For example, in Hawai'i, partly because it honors the American principle of the separation of church and state, religious tolerance, if not religious acceptance, has been a time-honored principle. Buddhist congregations, which comprise around twenty percent of the population in Hawai'i and which have been established entities for decades, have always been tolerated, if not openly supported, by the state. When it comes to religion in Hawai'i, "live and let live" seems to be the order of the day. With the more recent presence of Muslim communities, Mormon churches, New Age churches, religious sects, and native Hawaiian indigenous religious practices on the religious landscape of Hawai'i, religious pluralism and tolerance seem to be embedded now more than ever before in the Hawaiian Islands.

However, even though on the surface, religious tolerance seems to be a valued principle in the life and cultures of Hawai'i, a measure of

16. Commanger, *Documents of American History*, 8th ed., 124–25.

intolerance is being introduced into the society as the newer "successful" churches are becoming more established, both culturally and politically. This intolerance is evidenced in a number of ways, including a growing sentiment against homosexuality and the civil rights of those who are gay and lesbian, and also a recent protest originating in one church against an effort to promote inter-faith dialogue in one of the leading private (historically church-based) schools of the community.

In spite of these indications of a growing religious intolerance, it remains true that countless people living in Hawai'i still value the importance of religious tolerance. At the same time, it is also true that Christendom has indeed been an important ingredient in the history and culture of Hawai'i and that its vestiges are still with us. Although Christianity has not been a *legally* established religion in the United States or in Canada for over 200 years, it has nonetheless enjoyed a *cultural* establishment. That has also been true in Hawai'i. The fact of this cultural establishment of Christianity was described brilliantly first by Peter Berger in his 1961 book, *The Noise of Solemn Assemblies*, and by many others since then. The fact that Christianity did not achieve a legally sanctioned status did not prevent its establishment as the guiding religion of the culture. The life of Christian churches in the North American context has been tied to ways of the culture and *vice versa*. Both churches and the culture have shared a belief in progress with its attendant optimism; the notion of success measured by "bigness" and numbers; the importance of individualism and individual piety; and what has been construed to be the characteristics that constitute conventional, personal morality—honesty, hard work, family cohesiveness, sexual purity, and the like.

There was a time when one could not expect to achieve success in the society unless one was a member of an established church, preferably Protestant. That has changed. It is no longer assumed that the political and corporate leaders of the nation will be members of established mainline churches. Those days are gone. Yet, affiliation with a Christian church, usually of a conservative orientation, is still seen as an asset for those who want to be elected to political office.

In the past and in the present, there has been in Hawai'i a strong *unofficial* alignment between Christianity and the state, due in large part to Hawai'i's missionary past. Ever since the Congregational missionaries from New England landed on these island shores in the 1820s and converted most of the indigenous population to Christianity, deference among political authorities has always been given to Christian churches. This was true when mainline Protestant and Roman Catholic churches were prominent religious communities within Hawaiian society, and it is true today even as these mainline churches have been supplanted by newer, mostly evangelical and conservative Protestant churches (one even boasting a membership of ten- to eleven thousand people). Today, one cannot imagine a civic gathering in which a Christian minister does not play a major role, even though representatives of other religious traditions are also at such gatherings. And although the State Legislature opens each session with a prayer from a religious leader, most of those prayers are given by Christian pastors. Indeed, the Christian influence in Hawai'i's context has been so pervasive that Buddhist temples have found it necessary to pattern themselves according to the model of Christian churches.

Secularism has taken hold in Hawai'i as it has elsewhere on the North American continent, and a smaller and smaller percentage of the population attends churches and temples these days as compared with days past. Sunday mornings have become a time for soccer and shopping. At the same time, in the culture as a whole and in the political life of Hawai'i (one could hardly imagine a political fundraising event without an opening religious blessing), deference is still given to religious institutions in general, and Christian institutions in particular, with one exception, that being the older mainline Protestant churches.

Leaders and groups representing mainline Protestant churches continue to make public statements in support of same-sex marriage and civil rights to no avail. The one exception in a long line of failures has been the success in preventing the institution of state-sponsored gambling, but this is probably due to the fact that Roman Catholics, liberal Protestants and evangelicals have joined forces on this issue. For the most part, mainline Protestant voices count for very little. Yet, these same mainline Protestant religious leaders often do not seem to recognize that anything has changed. They still speak as though it were the 1960s when their voices were heeded. Today, although a certain amount of deference is still given to religious leaders from mainline Protestant communities, in reality these leaders have been pushed to the periphery of social and political life. This seems to be less true in the case of Roman Catholic leaders. In recent years, a growing alliance between the Roman Catholic Church and evangelical churches arising from their shared opposition to a woman's right to choose and equal marriage rights for same-sex couples has given strength to pronouncements by the Roman Catholic Diocese.

It used to be that everyone knew about the existence of Church of the Crossroads. Crossroads had achieved a certain reputation, or perhaps I should say notoriety, in the community because of its support of radical social causes. Now, when one says that he or she is a member of Church of the Crossroads, one must often explain just what this particular congregation is all about.

An example from the history of the congregation will suffice. Nearly forty years ago, Church of the Crossroads provided sanctuary to some thirty US soldiers who were AWOL because of their opposition to the Vietnam War. The church found itself the center of attention as the public, the media, the military police, and the FBI descended upon it. Its decision to provide sanctuary to the soldiers made headline news in the Honolulu papers. Even the British Broadcasting Corporation dispatched a team of filmmakers and reporters to do a documentary on this remarkable event.

This was important news because even forty years ago, the Protestant church still occupied a central place in the culture of Hawai'i. For a church to be so bold in its action drew lots of attention from the culture. Today, if Church of the Crossroads were to engage in the same kind of action, one wonders how much the world around it would care. In 2004, when this same church declared its support of same-sex marriages and sent out news releases to announce its decision, not one newspaper picked up on the story.

Whether the people of mainline Protestant churches want to believe it or not, their institutions have been pushed to the margins of the society. They no longer occupy a central position in the life of the culture surrounding them. Unlike the financial institution E. F. Hutton, when these churches speak, no one listens!

THE ATTEMPT TO RECOVER WHAT HAS BEEN LOST

From my observation of the religious scene in Hawai'i, especially of the churches of my own denomination, the United Church of Christ, there is a desperate attempt among the once-established churches of Protestantism to regain the prominence they once enjoyed. Many of them have become imitators of the style and often the message of the successful churches of the Christian right, the so-called megachurches. These churches of the Christian right have abandoned the obvious fundamentalist rhetoric of their pasts (although the spirit of fundamentalism is there, just under the surface), and have taken on the trappings of popular North American culture.

The worship style is often difficult to distinguish from entertainment. The music mirrors the more benign popular musical forms to be found in the culture. That may be a natural outcome of the effort to communicate the Gospel to a new generation. More problematic for me, however, is the fact that the words of the songs and hymns often betray a simplicity that does not take into account the profound experience of despair and meaninglessness and the struggle between faith and doubt, both of which belong to the human and faith experience of so many in our culture. Furthermore, the outreach techniques of the newer churches partake of the spirit of consumerism. A workshop promoted by an umbrella organization for conservative evangelical churches in Hawai'i not too long ago sponsored a workshop for churches and faith-based initiatives entitled *Serving Your Customer*.

The life of the newly established Christian churches is characterized by an absence of struggle, questioning, and ambiguity. Simple answers are provided to questions that, if explored deeply, could turn out to be complex questions indeed. Worshipers are often provided with sheets that outline the simple main points of the sermon with some space for personal reflections. Theological depth in these churches is avoided and a critical-historical approach to scripture is absent.

These newly established churches in Hawai'i are having an incredible influence on the once-mainline Protestant churches. A number of churches belonging to the United Church of Christ, anxious to increase their memberships, now follow plans for church growth that are promoted by megachurches such as the Willow Creek Church. All of these efforts speak of an evangelism fueled by a longing for numbers and success and a desire to be powerful and dominant players in the culture.

In churches that follow the prescriptions for success offered by the megachurches, there is hardly any distinction at all between the message of the Gospel and the trappings of popular, conventional culture with its allegiance to individualism and personal happiness. I have often thought that the message that is preached from the pulpits of these churches and the lessons that are taught to their members are akin to the kinds of advice one might find in the many books located in the self-help section of any bookstore.

I suspect that the churches that comprise the new Christian establishment would not agree with my analysis. They would point to their moral standards, most notably their opposition to homosexuality and abortion, and also their upholding of traditional family values, as positions that place them in opposition to popular culture.

Undoubtedly, there would be some truth to their response. Yet, I suspect that even in their moral stances, the churches of the Christian right tend to *reflect* widely held cultural attitudes rather than *stand apart* from them. For example, I have often thought that they have taken on the widespread homophobia present in the culture and have tried to give it a biblical basis, a basis, I might add, that is attached to just four or five questionable verses of scripture. As far as we know, Jesus had nothing to say on the subject.

The same tendency of churches to reflect the values of the surrounding culture may also hold true when it comes to the promotion of "traditional family values." In the culture, there is a fear that things are falling apart, including the structure of the family itself. This fear is present not only among Christians but also among many others, including those who are members of the social work community. The more conservative churches have captured this fear and given it prominence by holding on to and loudly proclaiming values that they consider traditional and biblically based. This places them in the mainstream of the culture rather than on the periphery of the culture. As regards the opposition of the churches of the Christian right to a woman's right to choose, I suggest that here too, their position reflects a growing perception in the wider culture, even among a majority who uphold a woman's right to make decisions about her own body, that abortion should be a means of last resort to end a pregnancy and that it is always problematic for a woman. Apart from these moral stances, however, the newer successful churches surely reflect the consumerism, the love of entertainment, and the passion for self-help solutions so obvious in our society, as well as the success orientation and individualism of the officially optimistic North American culture.

My intention here is not to put down these newer churches, even though they most assuredly represent the move to create a new kind of Christendom. Undoubtedly, they serve the perceived spiritual needs of many people in our society. Furthermore, one can only admire the skill and sophistication with which these churches are being established. The problem, as I see it, is the express intent of these newer churches to establish a new kind of Christendom, culturally and often legally. One must ask whether this effort to establish a new Christendom is a good thing or not.

In the United States, if not in Canada, the desire of the churches of the Christian right to seek a cultural establishment and even a limited legal establishment is obvious. Although they still run into roadblocks when they try to obtain legal sanction for their issues, they are succeeding culturally. It is said, and there is little reason to doubt it, that sixty million Americans were ready to vote for the re-election of George Bush simply because he described himself as an evangelical Christian. In American culture, it seems, Christianity is alive and well. Although many churches resist this effort to establish a new Christendom, many mainline Protestant churches are being tempted to follow the prescriptions that have accounted for the newfound success of churches belonging to the Christian right.

One, however, must ask: *Given the history of Christendom, its abuses, its distortion of the Gospel, its departure from the life and ministry and spirit of Jesus the Christ, and its abandonment of a theology of the cross in favor of a theology of glory, is a new Christendom anything Christians should desire?*

As I stated at the beginning of this chapter, I am suggesting another option for the mainline churches of Protestantism. I am proposing that our mainline churches actually embrace the process of disestablishment and see it as a blessing. This proposal invites our mainline churches to live with considerable ambiguity in their life and mission, simply because even as we are being disestablished, the vestiges of Christendom are still with us and not easily discarded. At the same time, this proposal to embrace the process of disestablishment presents our churches with an opportunity to find their way through this awkward moment in their history by returning to the original spirit of the Christian movement. That movement begun in the name of Jesus was centered in the reign of God and the cross of Christ rather than enamored with patterns of worldly success and power. It did not seek the "way of establishment" but sought only to know and proclaim "Jesus Christ, and him crucified" (1 Cor 2:2).

Having now placed the present-day church in context, I will proceed to tell the story of Church of the Crossroads, its history, its life, its ministry, and its witness. It is a story that speaks of a people who are embracing the process of disestablishment they are undergoing and who are consequently experiencing in their life together ambiguity as well as clarity, uncertainty as well as possibility, awkwardness as well as resolve, and hesitation as well as boldness of thought and action.

2

The Shaping of a Church

When we review the history of Crossroads, I believe it is important to take a close look at the people who founded this church. The fellowship was very young, mostly intermediate and high school students, with a sprinkling of some college students and then some people from—it was then the Evangelical Association—who had this idea of creating a church from a group of young people. Can you just imagine that happening today? The hopes, the dreams, the inspiration that went into the founding of this church, for me, all these make for an important legacy, and sometimes we lose sight of that.

—Kikue Takagi

From the beginning, Crossroads grew out of a sense of doing a new thing, and also doing a thing that was the right thing to do, and also doing something that others could look at and say, "Well, that's a huge thing for a small group to do." We are still a small group but we tend to act like we're a bigger church, in being and thinking about things. Perhaps that's part of our legacy. But I personally love to think back on that history, and just celebrate the courage and inspiration and the foresight of those young people who came together and founded this church.

—Linda Rich

I think much credit goes to Galen Weaver, his deep thinking, his broad-minded thinking. I'm not sure, but I don't think there is a church that has the different religions represented right by the pulpit such as we have here—Buddhism, Hinduism, Judaism, Zoroastrianism—anyway, I like to point out that we try to get along with all the other faiths. I think much credit goes to Galen Weaver's *understanding of humans and the broad thinking that helped build the foundation of Crossroads.*

—Shizuko Mukaida

The reason why I really joined this church was that I was in Japan and my wife Frances wrote to me telling me about the Sanctuary, and I thought, "That's my church," because I was very much opposed to the Vietnam War.

—Val Viglielmo

I know that the values of this church are based on peace, and I remember members talking about the church providing Sanctuary during the Vietnam War. I did not realize what a big deal that was until I was older. "Sanctuary" was just a word to me, and then as I got older, I understood that must have been a difficult stance to take in the community.

—Cathy Sox

It's an honor for me to be here—amongst the living—in this community that is Crossroads. It's an honor to be here amongst friends and teachers who are so down-to-earth and also so engaged in the good fight in this world. It's an honor to be part of this historic church in Hawai'i which has been such a vital gathering place for people and such a strong witness for justice and peace in these islands and our larger community. I'm honored also to be amongst the kupuna in our midst—it was Adelaide Kimura and her young peers who first came together over eighty years ago to create this new church and invest it with its identity. And as we know, they chose the coolest name—Church of the Crossroads. This church has pretty much lived up to its name in these islands. Crossroads has been a place where people of all different backgrounds and experiences are welcomed, can find common ground and share a common sense of purpose and calling. Crossroads has been a place where the weary and those with heavy burdens can lay them down, find healing and support, and be renewed to move a little more lightly through life. Crossroads has been a place with its doors open to the fresh winds of many struggles and movements through the years, giving Crossroads the character to persevere and keep being relevant to our present age.

—Mark Hamamoto, from a sermon "To Galilee" preached April 24, 2005

The Shaping of a Church

But now thus says the Lord,
he who created you, O Jacob,
he who formed you, O Israel;
Do not fear, for I have redeemed you;
I have called you by name, you are mine.
When you pass through the
waters, I will be with you;
and through the rivers, they
shall not overwhelm you;
when you walk through fire you
shall not be burned,
and the flame shall not consume you.
(Isa 43:1–2)

INTRODUCTORY REMARKS

MY INTENTION IN THE first chapter of this book was to describe two defining events in the history of the Christian Church: the establishment of Christendom and its ongoing disestablishment. I believe these two events largely account for the present context in which mainline churches, both Protestant and Catholic, find themselves. In this chapter, I want to introduce you, the reader, to Church of the Crossroads by tracing the major events and themes of its history as a congregation. I will not attempt to provide a detailed history of this particular congregation. That history can be found in two documents: the first a book, *The Crossroads Witness*, written by Betty Hemphill with Robert Hemphill, and the second a history written for the seventy-fifth anniversary of the church, *Living Between the Ideal and the Actual*, by Judy Rantala. Rather, my purpose here is to draw upon the history in order to interpret it in a way that illuminates the subject of this book, namely, that we now find ourselves between a Constantinian Christianity and a Christianity that is to be. We are, in a very real sense, a "Church *at a* Crossroads."

I say *a* Christianity that is to be, because as in the past, so in the future, Christianity will take on many forms and expressions. There will be a variety of Christian churches, groups and entities. As in days gone by, some of those churches will be large and successful. Others will be less notable, finding themselves more and more on the periphery of society rather than at its center. Of these, a few may choose to remain on the periphery. They will see that being on the edge of society gives them a greater freedom to participate more fully in the kingdom movement begun by Jesus, and through that participation they will be able to enter into a more meaningful dialogue with the society around them. Their freedom will be made possible simply because they will no longer be as subject to the limitations of being part of a religious establishment, most notably the limitation which comes from having to reflect the individualism, the optimism, and the success orientation of American society.

This book is being written for congregations that may want to choose this alternative path. It is not that these few will be any less important in light of God's realm. It may even be that they will be more able to bring the Gospel to bear upon the real needs of the society, for inasmuch as they will be communities of contrast in the world, they will be able to be in dialogue with the world simply because they are different. If there is no difference between the church and the world, there can be no dialogue. Of course, we cannot know what shape the Christian Movement will take in the future. We can only be open to the leading of the Spirit. There are, at the same time, pointers or signposts along the way, gifts of the Spirit that may shed light upon the path that Christian communities may want to take as they seek to pattern themselves after the "thin" tradition of *theologia crucis*, the theology of the cross.

As I reflect on the history of Church of the Crossroads, the congregation that now gathers on University Avenue in Honolulu near the University of Hawai'i, I am struck by two major themes that have been present from the beginning. On the one hand, the history of Church of the Crossroads has reflected the major trends and themes present in the course of liberal Protestantism in the North American context during much of the last century. On the other hand, the history of this particular community contains a number of departures from those trends and themes. These departures in themselves may not be all that remarkable except for those who experienced them. Perhaps they could more accurately be described as a foreshadowing of possible choices churches might make in our day if they should decide to become part of a Christian movement rather than seek to become re-established institutions.

As I review the history of Church of the Crossroads, I invite you to pay particular attention to those events and stances that placed this particular congregation on the edge of social and political life. These, I believe, have contributed to the congregation's desire to be intentional as it lives out its life, ministry, and mission in this present time of transition between the Christendom that dominated the past and a more faithful future.

BEGINNINGS

In a very real sense, the beginnings of Church of the Crossroads reflected the organizing patterns of many American Protestant liberal churches. The congregation was founded in 1923, and its founding covenant was one that typically reflected the theological principles of liberal Congregationalism.

> The covenant in which the members of this church join as their declaration of common faith and loyalty follows:
>
> We believe in and worship one God, most holy, most loving, and most free, whose character and purpose for men and women have been adequately made known in the filial and sacrificial love of Jesus Christ.
>
> We believe it is the divine purpose to establish upon the earth a universal society of the children of God devoted to a life of mutual respect and good will.
>
> We are united in striving to know the will of God and in our purpose to walk in the ways of the Lord, made known or to be made known to us.
>
> We hold it to be the mission of the Church of the Crossroads to proclaim the gospel to all people, to exalt the worship of the one true God, and to labor for the progress of knowledge, the promotion of justice, and the reign of peace, and the realization of human fellowship.
>
> We dedicate ourselves and the activities of this church to this cause. Through worship and common purpose, we seek mutual encouragement, growing understanding and fuller consecration.[1]

Similar covenants could surely be found in the historical documents of other Congregational churches organized in the first decades of the twentieth century. Yet, the founding of this church represented a departure from the mainstream, for it was organized as a multicultural church for the children of mostly Chinese and Japanese immigrants who had come to Hawai'i to find a better life for themselves and their families. An additional noteworthy feature about its beginning is that Crossroads was

---

1. The covenant was formulated in 1923 and revised in 1992 in an attempt to make the language gender neutral.

organized not only as a multicultural church but as a church for young people. Its first members were students from the Mid-Pacific Institute, a private high school begun by the Congregational Church for children of mainly Asian ancestry, and also students from McKinley High School, a public high school located on the corner of King and Pensacola Streets in Honolulu. Established Caucasian families, many of whom were descendants of Congregational missionaries, sent their children instead to the more prestigious Punahou School or, if they were members of the Episcopal Church, to Iolani School.

In keeping with its founding vision, over the years the church has included people from a number of racial and ethnic heritages. The multicultural heritage of Crossroads has been celebrated recently in two new banners hung in the sanctuary that use fabrics reflecting the diverse cultural backgrounds of the members.

On the one hand, then, Church of the Crossroads was founded as a church rooted in mainstream liberal Protestantism. On the other hand, it was a different kind of church. The fact that it was founded as an interracial congregation might seem to be a natural event in the context of Hawai'i. After all, Hawai'i for the past one hundred fifty years has been known as a multicultural society. To have been founded as an interracial congregation would have been an unusual, if not impossible, event in the Protestant world of the continental US in the 1920s. Yet, at the time it was also unusual in Hawai'i. In fact, Church of the Crossroads was the first interracial, intercultural Protestant church to be organized in Hawai'i. The other churches belonging to the Hawaiian Evangelical Association of the Congregational Christian Church, as well as other mainline Protestant denominations, had been founded along ethnic lines. There were Japanese churches, Native Hawaiian churches, *haole* (Caucasian) churches, and Chinese churches, but there were no Protestant churches embracing a number of ethnic heritages.

The name of the church in itself is significant. Church of the Crossroads was a name given by Frank S. Scudder and chosen deliberately to indicate the identity and purpose of this new congregation. Church of the Crossroads would seek to be just that, a "crossroads" between the university and the community, between East and West, between races and religions, and between the Gospel and the world.

The Shaping of a Church

THE LEGACY OF GALEN WEAVER

It was surely a remarkable beginning for a church. That beginning was nurtured and it flowered under the leadership of the founding pastor, Galen Weaver. It is said that the spirit of this remarkable man still hovers about the place and that he continues to influence the life and ministry of Crossroads. Long-time members of the church recall how Galen Weaver came to be at Crossroads. A graduate of Union Theological Seminary, he came to Hawai'i when he was only twenty-seven years old. As Kikue Takagi, a member, recalls, his original intent in coming through Hawai'i was to go to China as a missionary. Galen Weaver, like others of his generation, was fully committed to the missionary enterprise. He had been fired by the vision of the Student Volunteer Movement and its hope to "win the world for Christ in this generation." Weaver stopped in Hawai'i long enough for the Hawaiian Evangelical Association to persuade him to become the organizing minister of the little congregation of students that had come into being. He would remain with the congregation for twenty-seven years. Galen Weaver was an amazing human being. He was a good preacher and teacher, and a wonderful pastor. He read widely. He was acquainted with world religions. He was interested in drama and in music. He invited notable church leaders from many parts of the world to stop in Hawai'i on their travels and speak to the members of the church.

Galen Weaver reflected the best of the American liberal Protestantism of the time, and yet he also took stances that placed Church of the Crossroads on the edge of the mainstream of Hawaiian society. One story suffices. Elsie Ho, a founding member of the church, once recalled, "Hawai'i was controlled by the Big Five[2] and the plantations completely controlled their people. The housing was deplorable. Weaver sympathized with and supported the struggles of organized labor."[3]

How significant Weaver's sympathy for laborers was becomes obvious from historian Lawrence Fuchs' description of the class structures that prevailed in Hawai'i at the time.

---

2. The Big Five were: C. Brewer and Co., sugar, ranching, and chemicals, founded in 1826; Theo. H. Davies & Co., sugar, investments, insurance, and transportation, founded in 1845; Amfac (American Factors) Inc., sugar, insurance, and land development, founded in 1849; Castle and Cooke Inc. (Dole), pineapple, food packing, and land development, founded in 1851; and Alexander and Baldwin, Inc., shipping, sugar, and pineapple, founded in 1895. These five corporations ruled the economic life of Hawai'i for decades.

3. Elsie Ho, interview, March 29, 1982.

> No community of comparable size on the mainland was controlled so completely by so few individuals for so long. Rarely were political, economic, and social controls simultaneously enforced as in Hawaii. Rarely were controls so personal, and rarely were they as immune from such counterforces in Eugene Deb's socialism, Woodrow Wilson's New Freedom and Franklin D. Roosevelt's New Deal as in Hawaii. For forty years, Hawaii's oligarchy skillfully and meticulously spun its web of control over the Islands' politics, labor, land, and economic institutions, without fundamental challenge.[4]

For Galen Weaver, taking a stand against the controlling political and social elite of the community and standing in solidarity with the Japanese and Filipino plantation workers who were engaged in a struggle to form a labor union was a courageous act and "against the tide," for Crossroads had itself been dependent on the goodwill of the same elite. The members of the elite were mostly descendants of missionary families, some of whom had supported the founding of Crossroads with both money and involvement. The surnames of Wilcox, Richards, Castle, and Cooke are found among the early financial contributors to the young congregation, although most usually it was the *women* of these families who were behind the gifts!

The members of Church of the Crossroads supported Weaver's stand. Among these, John and Aiko Reinecke were most clearly connected with the labor movement. The Reineckes befriended Jack Hall and other union leaders who began to organize the plantation workers. As a result, John Reinecke lost his job as a teacher at McKinley High School and he and his wife were later charged with participating in "un-American activities." The support of Galen Weaver and Church of the Crossroads is remembered and honored to this day by the International Longshoremen's and Warehousemen's Union (ILWU) Local 137, the union that successfully organized the workers.

It was not only in the area of labor relations that Galen Weaver was a bold and gifted leader. He was keenly interested in interfaith dialogue, and he encouraged the members of Crossroads to study the religions of the world and to compare the lives of Buddha, Socrates, and Christ. In 1928, the members of the church staged an outdoor religious pageant, "The Light of the World: A Pageant of Man's Quest for God and God's

---

4. Fuchs, *Hawaii Pono: A Social History*, 152.

Quest for Man." The episodes depicted the Chinese emperor worshipping at the Altar of Heaven, Muslims praying to Allah, Buddhists meditating, Hindus proud of their ancient religious heritage, and the Hebrew faith flowering in the prophets. At the close,

> The Interpreter leads all to the light that is in Jesus Christ, "The Light of the World." Together they move, at the beckon of childhood and youth, to a great common faith, in which nothing good is lost, but all values are fulfilled.[5]

The pageant reveals something about the spirit of Crossroads that one can still detect today. Church of the Crossroads is Christocentric in its life and ministry, and yet it values and honors the truths of other religious traditions and desires a world in which nothing that is good and worthy in those traditions will be lost.

Throughout his ministry, Galen Weaver always emphasized the importance of "thinking the faith," and this too has been important for the congregation throughout the years. In 1927, he expressed this passion in a letter to Theodore Richards, and yet he also emphasized in that same letter the need for action.

> I do believe that Christians today do too little thinking. We ignore the great body of established knowledge to our peril. What we need to emphasize along with open-mindedness is the spiritual imperative to act on the faith we have, growing into larger faith, partly by clear thinking, but even more *by courageous acting* . . .[6]

The necessity of keeping alive the dialectic between thought and action is a theme to which I will return later as I describe some of the present struggles of the congregation.

There are many other ways in which Galen Weaver encouraged the people of Crossroads to embark upon new and different paths. Yet, I would be remiss if I did not also mention the faithful witness of the church during World War II. The days and years following the attack of Japan on Pearl Harbor were difficult indeed, but the one people who suffered the most were those of Japanese ancestry. The Japanese of Hawai'i did not suffer to the extent of the Japanese who lived on the mainland United States. Yet, it is sometimes forgotten that as many as 1,875 living in Hawai'i at the

---

5. Church of the Crossroads, *Fifth Anniversary Brochure*, 18.
6. Weaver, letter, May 2, 1927.

time were sent to mainland concentration camps, and others were also interned closer to home, in the cane fields above Pearl Harbor.

Church of the Crossroads reached out to the internees as well as the Japanese members of the larger community in a remarkable way. The church persuaded Alice Cary to come to Crossroads to organize the outreach. She had been born in Osaka of missionary parents, had received her education in the United States, and had then returned to Japan to teach at Kobe College and Doshisha University. After she worked in Siberia with the Red Cross, she again returned to Japan to work with the victims of the Great Earthquake of 1923 and then to organize a Christian social settlement in Osaka. Well-equipped for the task at hand, Alice Cary came to Crossroads in 1941. Along with Galen Weaver, Frank Scudder, and other members of Crossroads, she carried out a ministry of hospitality and encouragement to local Japanese families who were beset by fear and uncertainty. Said Weaver, "We are especially eager to talk with any who are disturbed by the present situation and who face special problems and difficulties."[7] The church's bulletin board was used to post helpful messages. The church office promised to report any incidents of discrimination and critiques of any discriminatory policies to the proper government authorities. The ministry of *justice* and *hospitality*, so important in the early years of Church of the Crossroads, would continue to guide the church in the years ahead and take it along new and challenging paths.

ARCHITECTURE

In the pattern of the newly organized Protestant churches of the time, Church of the Crossroads embarked on a building program. The first building to be designed and constructed was the sanctuary. It incorporated a traditional cruciform pattern, and at the same time represented a departure from traditional forms. Looking at the shape of the sanctuary from above, one would see the form of a cross, with a nave and chancel forming the upright portion of the symbol and the transepts, the horizontal crosspiece. In recent years, the transepts of the church have been put to proper use as places for people to sit, and so it is that now, when the community gathers for worship, the members, in bodily form, actually manifest the cross that is so central to the life of the One they seek to follow.

---

7. Quoted in Hemphill and Hemphill, *The Crossroads Witness*, 57.

The Shaping of a Church

Yet, there are elements in the architecture that depart from the traditional. Those who find themselves inside and outside the sanctuary of Central Union Church in Honolulu could be easily transported to a New England Congregational church, but those who approach and enter the sanctuary of Church of the Crossroads know they are in a space that is different from the ordinary. One notes the simplicity and "plainness" of the building, but wherever there is a measure of ornamentation, one sees native Hawaiian and Japanese motifs. The shape of the indigenous *lauhala* (pandanus) tree is carved into the stone inlays between the three front doors of the church. The red pillars framing the front porch of the church remind one of a Japanese *torii* (shrine gate). The cross on top of the church tower arises out of three rings symbolizing the multi-tiered umbrella used to shield an itinerant Buddhist monk from the sun and rain.

Inside the church, the eye focuses on the simple central cross on the altar. The pulpit extends outward from the boundary line of the chancel and lectern holding the Bible, indicating that the preacher was to be free to include other truths beside the truths of scripture in his or her preaching. Quickly noticeable are the wood carvings bordering the chancel. These were incorporated into the sanctuary when it was constructed in 1935. Utilizing a unifying symbol of a hand, the panels honor four religious traditions other than Christianity—from left to right, Zoroastrianism, Judaism, Buddhism, and Hinduism. The artist, Margaret Blasingame, said of her work: "Through all the carvings, the effort was made to express the mood of the emotional intensity of mystic introspection, but controlled, both intellectually and by the limitations imposed by the material and the architectural necessities."[8] That such an honoring of other religious traditions was incorporated in the architecture of a church building constructed in the mid-1930s is remarkable indeed. The "crossroads" theme was later incorporated in the additional buildings surrounding the central courtyard. Two of these buildings, Scudder and Ross-Davis, are distinctively Japanese in design. All of the buildings are connected by walkways or loggia featuring brilliant red pillars, and with the aqua-blue roofs of the buildings (they have now faded), the distinct impression is that of a Chinese temple.

In fact, I am told that a temple in northern China may have inspired Claude Albon Stiehl, at the time a well-known and respected architect in

---

8. Church of the Crossroads, *Twentieth Anniversary Brochure*, 18.

Hawai'i, as he designed the sanctuary and later Ross-Davis and Scudder. Stiehl's buildings, which include a number of homes, have taken their place among the architectural treasures of the state. The sanctuary itself was added to the official list of Hawai'i's historically treasured buildings in 1995.

DELWYN RAYSON AND THE 1960s

The post-WWII years at Church of the Crossroads followed the pattern of so many Protestant churches on the North American continent. The membership of the church increased significantly. At one time during the fifties, there were nearly seven hundred children in the church school! This memory speaks for itself. Yet, today, we rarely hear members speak as if they wished a return to those days. In fact, one rarely hears members talk about the 1950s at all! Clearly, these "successful" years did not shape the present spirit of the congregation.

Church of the Crossroads entered the turbulent sixties with the call of the Rev. Delwyn Rayson as its pastor. Rayson, along with Galen Weaver and later Anthony Robinson, is remembered to this day as a decisive influence in the shaping of Crossroads. Rooted in both the spirit of liberal Protestantism and the values of democratic socialism, Rayson, like Galen Weaver before him, advocated a thinking faith and a well-educated laity. A mild-mannered man in private, Rayson came alive in the pulpit and many from the wider community came to Crossroads to hear him preach. A little book of sermons collected in 1964 reveals much about Del Rayson. The sermons are filled with quotations from Dietrich Bonhoeffer, Sigmund Freud, Teilhard de Chardin, William Barrett, Paul Tillich, Martin Buber, George Santayana, Thomas Merton, T. S. Eliot, Samuel Beckett, Søren Kierkegaard, David Hume, C. S. Lewis, Albert Schweitzer, Martin Luther, newspaper articles, and a host of other sources. Multiple education courses using these same sources and many more were organized for church members, not only for adults but also for teenagers. Those who participated in these courses emerged as theologically articulate people in their own right.

To characterize the theology of Del Rayson, I would say that he advocated a worldly Christianity, and also a de-institutionalized Christianity. Ahead of his time, Rayson even spoke of the need for a post-Christendom church. In a sermon, "Faith without Religion," he said:

The Shaping of a Church

> . . . You could point out that, maybe, Christendom is the fundamental misfortune of Christianity, in the sense that when religious people accommodate God to culture, and, as Sam Miller says, corner Him ecclesiastically, teach Him their rules, train Him to bow to their ceremonial expectations, that then it is the faith itself which becomes unrecognizable and hardly worth the attention of serious people, and when this happens, life itself is betrayed to mediocrity. This is precisely what has happened in our secular world. It is religion itself which seems childish and inconsequential to increasing numbers of our college youth. And it isn't that they are really irreligious, but rather that they cannot relate their genuine hunger for meaning and purpose to the triviality and separatism and self-protectiveness which so often characterizes life in the religious institution.[9]

With a past that includes a voice like this, it is natural that today Church of the Crossroads should take the journey of becoming a post-Christendom church.

In October 1960, soon after he arrived on the scene, Rayson introduced to the congregation his concept of the servant church:

> (a) The church exists for others (for the service of those outside the Church, for the service of members only in the service of non-members);
>
> (b) The Church exists for mission (mission is its whole reason for being, ministry is the first job of every Christian).[10]

These principles, after much discussion and debate, were adopted in full by the congregation three years later. Rayson pinned his continuing ministry at Crossroads on congregational support for these principles. In a circular letter to family and friends written in early 1964, Rayson said,

> This has been a very decisive year for my ministry here. I have been pushing for a radical re-structuring of the church, for a concept of the church as a serving community willing to lose itself and to risk its resources in new forms of service in the world, in contradistinction to the traditional idea of the church as a separate religious institution, existing for itself apart from the structures and needs of the world. This is part of the very significant movement for church renewal throughout all churches. But it is now a vital issue here,

---

9. Rayson, *Faith in a World Come of Age*, 19.
10. Rayson, church document, October, 1960.

and a minority of our congregation have been resisting it, out of inner anxieties and fears, I feel. We are currently going through congregational meetings which will decide the issue and, I feel sure, give me the authority for even more radical experimentation.[11]

I have quoted the words of this letter in full because they reveal much about Del Rayson and his ministry. They speak of a radical understanding of the church that would later lead to the suggestion that, as an institution, the Church of the Crossroads should even cease to be once it had completely lost itself in the service of the world. Secondly, his letter speaks of the fears of some of the members that there would be a neglect of the pastoral dimension of congregational life. Service to others was to include service not to members, but only to non-members of the church. Thirdly, one senses the charismatic nature of Rayson's ministry. He was seeking a personal authority to carry out an "even more radical experimentation," almost as if the future of the church lay in his own hands rather than in the hands of the congregation itself.

These issues would not go away in the days to come, and the questions are still important. What kind of pastoral leadership is best for a congregation? Can there be a service to the world that does not neglect the ministry of love and care among the members of the church? If a church is to lose its life in the world, is the care and maintenance of the church buildings justified in any way? Does mission have only to do with what a church does in the world or does it also include the worship and communal life of the congregation itself?

Crossroads, though, did take Del Rayson's call to heart, and a most remarkable ministry to the students of the university was initiated. It culminated in turning Schenck Hall, one of the ancillary buildings of the church (actually the first meeting place of the congregation), into a coffeehouse offering tea, coffee, soup, and bread for twenty-five cents. It was self-governing and worked well for awhile until the alternative culture of the sixties began to exert a negative influence. A committee organized to study the matter recommended that the coffeehouse be shut down, but the recommendation was not accepted by the congregation. An official statement was adopted outlining the purpose of the coffeehouse.

> The purpose of the Coffeehouse is to encourage people to be freer and more loving by providing a place and atmosphere for inner

---

11. Rayson, letter dated January 8, 1964.

growth. It is a place where people can get together in order to better understand and accept themselves and their responsibility for others. It provides an accepting community that rejoices in diversity, encourages creativity and the free interchange of ideas.[12]

Two years later, on October 14, 1967, Honolulu police raided the coffeehouse, which by then was called The Freeway Coffee House, and arrested eighteen young men and women, charging them with either selling or possessing narcotics. When he was interviewed, Rayson commended the conduct of the police and added that he hoped the arrests would have a sobering effect and result in a reinforcement of the rules the church had established prohibiting the use of drugs and liquor in the house.

Clearly, Crossroads attempted to put Rayson's call to service into action, but it is also clear that Rayson desired even bolder action. At the same time, he had become disenchanted with the main currents of liberal Protestant theology and had adopted a death-of-God theology popularized by Thomas Altizer. Following a summer with the civil rights movement in the south and particularly the Delta Ministry in Mississippi, Rayson returned to Honolulu in August 1966, and preached his first sermon:

> I've just come back from my three months' leave to tell you the one more step which I think that we as a church must take in radical obedience to the gospel in our time. This is a difficult step, one easily misunderstood and readily maligned. We may even be called "atheist" if we take it. I mean the step of getting along without God! . . . God is not needed, the Church is not needed; religion is not needed. And to take this fact very seriously is the only way we can stand within the spirit of our times . . .[13]

A growing opposition to this new theology arose among the members of the congregation and Rayson resigned two years later in 1968. In the sermons Rayson preached towards the end of his tenure, one senses a growing impatience in this remarkable man whose influence is still remembered and respected by many members of Crossroads. Even the Sanctuary event that was to follow Rayson's ministry did not finally, in his estimation, satisfy his call to the church to lose itself in the service of the world. This is clear from a sermon which he preached in the early

---

12. Rayson, "A Statement to the Congregation on the Coffee House," June 13, 1965.
13. Rayson, "Jesus and the Beatles—Or, Where Do We Go From Here," sermon, August 21, 1966.

seventies upon a return visit to Crossroads. I will return to that sermon later after describing the Sanctuary event itself.

SANCTUARY

A couple of summers ago, a middle-aged man stood outside the door of my study and asked if he might go into the sanctuary of the church. I said "surely" and together we went out into the courtyard to join his wife and two children who were waiting on the porch of the sanctuary. I didn't ask him why he wanted to see the sanctuary, but as soon as he got inside and took a look, his eyes began to tear, and he said something like this, "You can never know how much this place means to me. You see, I was one of those soldiers who found a home here when there was no place else to go. The hospitality and kindness I received here changed my life and set me on a right path, and I wanted my family to come to Hawai'i with me so that they too could experience this special and sacred place."

Sometimes, when reviewing the significance of the Sanctuary event, called simply "Sanctuary" in the life of Church of the Crossroads, we remember the notoriety the event engendered but forget the *human* side of the event. In a thesis written about the Sanctuary event, Linda Tillich indicates that the soldiers who found a home at Crossroads were not of the upper class or even the middle class. They were men who had known the trials of growing up poor and on the edge. For many of them, this was the first time they sensed they were honored for who they were, and this affirmation gave them such a lift that they were able to move on in life with commitment and hope. The words of the former soldier who came back that day led me to understand that the Sanctuary event was as much a sign of hospitality as it was a courageous witness of social justice and peace on the part of the congregation.

The event itself occurred a year after Del Rayson departed. The congregation had taken his preaching about the "church in the world" seriously. Changes in the structure of the congregation were put in place to make a bold witness in the world more possible. Greater authority and decision-making power was vested in the Executive Board of the church. In its communal life, a variety of worship patterns were put in place that would "spring out of involvement in the world."[14] By this time, the political establishment had taken note of Church of the Crossroads and

---

14. Church of the Crossroads study paper, February, 1969.

its potential for disruptive behavior. The State Commission on Subversive Activities in its March 4, 1969 report labeled the church as an "activist" congregation. The Commission had been established in 1955 as a fact-finding body to identify individuals and groups engaged in subversive activities and it included in its report those belonging both to the "old left" and the "new left." Crossroaders were identified as "well-meaning but probably misguided citizens" being used by the radical left. Of course, the Executive Board of the church protested the findings, and the *Honolulu Star-Bulletin* came to the church's defense. An editorial said:

> The commission labors under the weight of a heavily-loaded word—"subversive." When it mentions anyone by name in that connection it ought to be *careful*. Yet the current report mentions names almost casually—even including the Church of the Crossroads, which has both a high quotient of idealism and a large number of respected University of Hawaii faculty members in its congregation. The church leaders have indeed provided a forum for those who believe that much is wrong with America, but when that becomes subversive, then America will be in big trouble.[15]

Truly, Church of the Crossroads some thirty-five years ago experienced what it meant to be "on the edge" and a minority community within a Christendom culture.

The leadership of Crossroads was undeterred. Finding itself opposed to much of what was going on in the society, most especially the Vietnam War, the Executive Board of the church in May 1968 proposed to the congregation that it offer draft counseling and "sanctuary for those who engage in nonviolent forms of resistance as a matter of conscience." There was a rumor that some local men stationed at Schofield Barracks might be sent to Vietnam and there was interest in a sanctuary. Seven months later, on December 11, 1968, the congregation ratified the proposal.

Kikue Takagi, a leader at the time, recalls that the church had no idea as to what might eventually take place. A measure of naiveté accompanied the resolution to offer Sanctuary. Perhaps, though, this too is a sign of what it means to be a community shaped by the cross. Such a community does what the Spirit calls it to do, not quite knowing what will happen. Seven months later on August 6, 1969, Airman Louis D. Parry arrived at the church seeking sanctuary. He did so because, as he

---

15. Editorial, *Honolulu Star Bulletin*, March 12, 1969.

said, he was ending his complicity with the US military and its crimes against humanity. Thirty-five servicemen, at one time or other, would seek refuge at Crossroads during the course of the next thirty-four days. The Sanctuary ended on September 12 at dawn when military police arrived on the campus, entered the buildings, and arrested the eight men who remained in residence.

I myself was not present at Crossroads during this time, but I have heard so many stories from so many people that it is as though this event has become part of my own experience. Kikue Takagi recalls:

> We were totally unprepared when the servicemen seeking sanctuary appeared. We had no plans for housing, meals, showers . . . The first few days were chaotic and no one was in charge. The Resistance moved in as did all kinds of unrelated, curious folk. The media, including the British Broadcasting Corporation and the NBC Network, reported the event, at times on a daily basis, and the police, the military and the FBI kept the grounds under constant surveillance. In retrospect, I wonder why the military allowed the Sanctuary to continue for five and a half weeks. By the time they came, most of the men had left the premises.

At one point, the agents of the FBI or CIA tried to enter the draft counseling office (now the pastor's study) to confiscate the files. Judy Rantala, a member of the church, asked one of the agents the purpose of their visit. "I want your files that are in the office," the agent replied. Rantala then asked, "Do you have an official search warrant?" "No," said the agent, "but I want your files." She stood at the door of the office, her hands braced against the two sides of the door frame, and refused to let the agents in. They were no match for Judy Rantala and they retreated! John Norris, also a member of the congregation, resigned from his military commission in protest of the war and as a sign of solidarity with the servicemen. The personal stories surrounding the event are numerous and should never be forgotten.

The Church gained notoriety overnight and little wonder. Others recall that the FBI even rented a room in the circular office building adjacent to the campus so that it could keep a watch on the place. The atmosphere took on the characteristics of a carnival. A kind of "messiness" prevailed. Toshiaki Suematsu, an eccentric builder of unusual structures from castaway materials and a favorite unofficial guru of students at the University of Hawai'i, arrived on the scene and built a tower made of odds and ends from which he hung a plumb line as a sign, he said, that

The Shaping of a Church

God was judging Church of the Crossroads. Toshi was well versed in the Bible and enjoyed discussing theological questions. During the days, Toshi made a home for himself on the church grounds. One day it was reported that the cross was missing from the altar. When it reappeared, it was explained that he, as a self-appointed guardian of the cross, had "stolen" it and hidden it for safekeeping.

Notable was the lack of any supportive presence from the clergy and members of other churches, although a few pastors from other denominations did come as a sign of solidarity. In fact, so many complaints about the Sanctuary flooded the headquarters of the United Church of Christ Conference office in Hawai'i that the congregation issued a statement reminding the churches of the Hawai'i Conference of the principle of local church autonomy and its accompanying freedom, and also asking for the prayers of all people.

On the fiftieth anniversary of the church, Del Rayson was asked to return to Crossroads to preach the sermon. In part, he said:

> Throughout much of its history, I feel sure, the Church of the Crossroads has also so understood the implications of its own faith. I remember preaching the fortieth anniversary sermon in 1963 and tracing a prophetic line of continuity from the past to the present. I was sinning then; and I misread the Church and its potential in at least two very serious respects.
>
> I did not realize how unable was the Church to move from the beauty of the Gospel's claim to some tangible achievement of justice and freedom in the world; how futile then and parochial and contradictory was its congregational medium against the grandeur of its own universal and timeless message.
>
> What I also did not understand, and I doubt many of us fully comprehend now, is the extent to which our best rhetoric and our most earnest strivings, were sadly compromised by our cultural captivity and political naiveté. This is a comment on our illusory pride as well, for while we quite rightly judged the self-serving cultural subservience of other churches like Central Union and Kawaiahao, we were blind to the more subtle forms our own social conformism was taking.[16]

In these words, Rayson mirrored the feelings of many members of the church that all the attempts to serve the world, even providing sanctuary to the AWOL servicemen, had not amounted to very much. In a way, he

16. Rayson, "Fiftieth Anniversary Sermon," May 20, 1973.

points to the illusions to which churches, even churches like Church of the Crossroads, are bound. Christendom and its theology of glory are not easily set aside. Rayson's words suggest that, for all of its activism, Crossroads was still caught up in the American cultural values of success and accomplishment. These were part and parcel of the values not only of churches that took the middle road and refrained from any kind of witness for peace and justice in the world, but also churches that were inspired by the prophetic spirit and the need for a strong witness in the world. What Rayson failed to realize, perhaps, was that the Sanctuary event may not have had much influence upon the world, but that, in itself, it was a sign of the church's faithfulness in the midst of an unjust war. He also failed to note that the Sanctuary event had meaning for the thirty-five soldiers who sought refuge at Crossroads, men such as the one who returned after all those years so that he, with his family in tow, could experience once again the special and sacred place that had transformed his life.

DARK AND DIFFICULT DAYS

The Sanctuary took a toll on Church of the Crossroads. The congregation lost many members because of the action, especially those of Japanese ancestry who felt that Crossroads in providing sanctuary had betrayed their deeply held value of loyalty to the nation. In addition, those who had been attracted to the church by the charismatic leadership and preaching of Del Rayson and also by the excitement of the Sanctuary days began to withdraw from active participation in the church.

A faithful remnant remained, but even these were divided between the supporters of the action and those who silently opposed the same. These two groups began to worship separately. The "progressives" gathered in the Ross-Davis Room, using a variety of worship patterns and styles, and the "traditionalists" gathered at the same time for worship in the sanctuary. Financial support for the church decreased and the upkeep of the buildings was neglected.

Still, the spirit of the sixties continued to prevail among the leadership of the church. It was decided that the congregation should structure itself to reflect more adequately a lay-led congregation in which the separation between clergy and laity would be dissolved. It was decided that the church did not really need a pastor after all, and so it chose to call a "Coordinator of Ministries" instead, a position defined as a counselor,

The Shaping of a Church

facilitator, and consultant, but not as a traditional pastor. Pastoral responsibilities would be handled by members of the congregation themselves. The Coordinator was to preach no more than once a month. Ironically, the search for the Coordinator of Ministries was limited to ordained clergy. In retrospect, of course, this was a course of action doomed to failure. Those who stayed with the congregation now realize that what was needed, more than ever before, was a pastor and teacher. The Rev. Arlie Porter was called to serve as the new Coordinator of Ministries. His tenure was filled with tension and controversy and disappointment.

Significant things took place, nonetheless. Remembering the commitment to "thinking the faith" established most especially in the ministries of Weaver and Rayson, it was decided to institute a Theologian-in-Residence program, and in 1970, Gabriel Fackre came as a teacher to be with the congregation. Later, in 1972, John B. Cobb came for a year to serve in the same capacity. Many years later, the congregation revived the Theologian-in-Residence program when Douglas John Hall came to be with the congregation in early 2003.

In his farewell sermon preached on July 29, 1973, in the midst of the conflicted congregation, John Cobb said something worth recalling. He noted the bondage of the congregation, evidenced by its nostalgia for the days of Weaver and Rayson and for the exciting experience of Sanctuary. He also drew attention to the sins of individualism, the resentment for past hurts, and the self-righteousness that now permeated the congregation. He expressed concern that the worship services so rarely contained "the note of confession and pardon" so necessary if the church was to move ahead.

In the mid-1970s, the congregation experienced its lowest point. Edith Laeha, a member of the church, remembers that one Sunday, only six people or so gathered for worship. One wonders what kept the church alive at all. Why did it not cease to be a church, as has been the fate of so many mainline Protestant churches in recent years? From my own point of view, I would say that Church of the Crossroads did not die because those who stayed with the church had come to experience Christian faith as a *movement* rather than an *establishment*. They also understood that the Christian movement needs to find its embodiment in *Christian community*, and so they refused to accept what appeared to be inevitable.

RENEWAL

In the late 1970s, there were signs that something new was about to take place. A realization began to grow that the church could not survive if it refused to change. The Rev. Gloria Kibbee, the first woman pastor in the history of Crossroads, was called in 1977. While she did her best to bring the congregation back together, she unfortunately died suddenly in 1980 and so did not have enough time to fulfill the promise of her ministry. Even so, there were significant moments in the life of the congregation that held the promise of renewal.

One such moment was a letter that Andrew Lind, a gifted sociologist at the University of Hawai'i and often a voice of reason within the congregation, presented to the congregation through its moderator.

> Crossroads had never during the greater part of the first fifty years of its history insisted on consensus theologically, intellectually, or in any other respect among all its members, and I don't think it should now. What has characterized Crossroads for so many years, and what probably attracted most of us in the first place, was the sincerity and openness of its approach, not only to the Bible and the Gospel of Jesus, but also to the world in which we live today and to all its problems. But the spirit of Crossroads, or what I would like to think has been its distinctive quality, has always sustained the conviction that no one of us (not even the minister) has the full measure of truth, but that we can more nearly approximate an understanding of the mysteries of life from those who share such an open and sincere approach to our common objectives.[17]

Lind proposed a serious effort each Sunday, between the two worship services, to bring together the two separate groups making up the Crossroads community through the means of an interchange of ideas on current issues of major import.

The promise of renewal was also evidenced in the beginning of a new ministry of music, which is still in place today. Don Conover, a skilled pianist and choir director, came to the church in 1976 and noticed the absence of a choir. He offered to organize one and did so, bringing together members of the congregation and interested folk from the wider community. Throughout the years, the choir has formed one of the most cohesive and caring groups in the church. The choir became a sign of

---

17. Lind, letter to moderator Teruo Sasaki, March 1978.

the kind of community that would one day be more fully realized in the whole of the congregation.

Following the death of Gloria Kibbee, the congregation entered into a fairly lengthy search for a new pastor that culminated in the calling of the Rev. Anthony Robinson in 1980. Along with Weaver and Rayson, Tony Robinson is remembered as one of the pastors who did much to shape the spirit of Church of the Crossroads. To the position, he brought skills in preaching, teaching, and the pastoral ministry. The thought of renewal now resided among many in the congregation, and Robinson provided the necessary leadership to bring it about. During his ministry, the congregation once again came together in a single worship service. To this day, the members of Crossroads resist any thought of a second service. Moreover, a pattern of worship based on the liturgical renewal movement encouraged by the Council on Church Union (COCU) and incorporated in a new *United Church of Christ Book of Worship* became the unifying pattern of worship for the congregation. Not fully appreciated by everyone, this pattern of worship has nonetheless persisted through the years and has, in my estimation, done much to provide a spirit of unity among the members of the congregation.

Robinson is also remembered as an insightful teacher and theologian. In this connection, he brought to his ministry a strong commitment to the importance of scripture. Following the suggestion of Yale theologian George Lindbeck and others, he firmly believed that the life of the congregation and the individual lives of its members would be enriched if sufficient attention was paid to the meta-narratives of the Bible. Utilizing the discipline of the Common Lectionary, his preaching reflected his own deep immersion in the study of scripture. In a sermon preached on November 18, 1985, Robinson reviewed all the various theological positions found in the Crossroads community, and then he described the congregation this way:

> I would argue that a much more adequate description of Crossroads' theological identity than "open" and "diverse" is the following: Church of the Crossroads is a theologically pluralistic congregation with a bias in favor of Biblical prophetic religion and its understanding of Christian faith as a critique of a fallen world and witness to God's transforming purposes. This statement would certainly not go uncontested within the congregation. . . .

> Nevertheless, I believe it is essentially faithful to the past and present, and that it gives a direction for the future.

Then, Robinson offered a proposal for life and accountability in such a pluralistic congregation.

> The three lines of accountability are to Scripture, to the community (the church) and to lived experience. Of these, I judge Scripture to have a pre-eminent place as the collective story and distinctive world view of this community.[18]

During Robinson's tenure, the membership increased, a church school was organized largely due to the efforts of Linda Robinson, his wife, and the congregation became once again a community of hope.

CHOOSING A PERSPECTIVE

The story will end here for the time being. The history of the late 1980s and the 1990s will be reflected elsewhere in this book. As one reviews the history of this particular congregation, questions arise. What can we learn from the history of our churches? What perspective ought we to take as we review the past? Here, I am reminded of something that Kikue Takagi related as she recalled the dark and difficult days of the 1970s in the life of the congregation. Years ago, she found herself describing those difficult years to a visiting denominational staff person. After listening to her, he said something like this: "Never forget the difficult times in the life of the church because those are the times when the possibilities for change and new understandings can emerge."

I would agree. It is when the members of Church of the Crossroads, or any church, for that matter, remember the difficult times that they will be encouraged in their faithfulness in the present. For insight and wisdom and courage are given rarely in the midst of success. Far more often, they are given in the midst of trial.

I suspect that most churches belonging to a mainline liberal Protestant past remember the days when they were "successful" churches, when their pews were filled and their church school classrooms were overflowing. Perhaps that is necessary if they want to re-establish themselves as churches of the majority. On the other hand, should they choose to be churches shaped not by a theology of glory but by a theology of

---

18. Robinson, "Identity and Pluralism at The Crossroads," November 18, 1985.

the cross, it would be far better for them to recall the times when their churches found themselves on the edge, on the periphery of society.

The events and stances in the history of Church of the Crossroads that placed it on the edge of society reveal a congregation that has been *unwilling* at times to simply mirror the conventional and acceptable forms of church life that characterized the American Protestantism of the last century. I believe those dissonant events and risk-filled stances in the congregation's past have encouraged and set it free to live in the present, as uncertain and awkward as it is, with a certain measure of authenticity as it moves away from its Christendom past and towards a more faithful future.

As I have considered the history of Church of the Crossroads, I have therefore chosen to recall the times when the church stood apart from the majority, when the church chose to be a different kind of community, when the church took on the cost of faithful discipleship, when the church risked its own life for the sake of others, and then when, as a consequence, the church itself suffered and came very close to the real possibility of its own demise. For it was then, in all of its vulnerability and weakness, that the spirit of the crucified Christ and the grace of God entered into its life and brought forth a measure of hope and newness. I cannot help but turn to words the Apostle Paul wrote to the Church in Corinth:

> . . . we proclaim Christ crucified, a stumbling block to Jews and foolishness to Gentiles, but to those who are the called, both Jews and Greeks, Christ the power of God and the wisdom of God. For God's foolishness is wiser than human wisdom, and God's weakness is stronger than human strength.
>
> Consider your own call, brothers and sisters: not many of you were wise by human standards, not many were powerful, not many were of noble birth. But God chose what is foolish in the world to shame the wise; God chose what is weak in the world to shame the strong; God chose what is low and despised in the world, things that are not, to reduce to nothing things that are, so that no one might boast in the presence of God (1 Cor 1:23–29).

This is the kind of word from scripture that has the power to sustain Christian communities who wish to take on the cost as well as the joy of discipleship, who wish to recognize the weakness of their witness and also their vulnerability as they seek to engage the world. It is to that engagement with the world that I will next turn my attention.

3

Engaging the World

I find myself sort of compulsively reading both newspapers and watching television news—not only corporate US media news broadcasts but also NPR and the British Broadcasting Corporation because I think it's so helpful for us to hear a different national perspective on what we're doing and what we look like. . . . I certainly feel some fear and I have a sense that we're moving in a very frightening direction. . . . I am just horrified at some of the things that are being disclosed and at the same time I am so grateful for the courageous people who are disclosing some of those things. . . . I am also, in the face of all that is really happening, very hopeful because I see some people speaking out very courageously. . . . Even in our church, I see more action happening around issues in the world we need to address openly and publicly, and that's very exciting. So my feelings are really mixed. . . . I find myself horrified, fearful, sad, and at the same time moved when I see tremendous courage in the people who are standing up and speaking and acting.

—Linda Rich

It's a world of disparities and exploitation, disparities between the rich and the poor within countries, and between rich and poor countries, and also widening gaps between rich and poor, and the exploitation of the poor by the rich. . . . It's something like the economic pattern of neo-colonialism.

—Ryland Moore

As Christians and as Crossroaders, if we pay serious attention to Jesus, we could really influence the world around us based on what Jesus would really do. I see this beginning to happen with our ministries of

Engaging the World

peace, justice, and the stewardship of creation. I believe that Christ is working through us to make a difference in the wider world.

—Judy Fiocco

As they were going along the road, someone said to him, "I will follow you wherever you go." And Jesus said to him, "Foxes have holes, and birds of the air have nests; but the son of Man has nowhere to lay his head." To another he said, "Follow me." But he said, "Lord, first let me go and bury my father." But Jesus said to him, "Let the dead bury their own dead; but as for you, go and proclaim the kingdom of God." Another said, "I will follow you, Lord; but let me first say farewell to those at my home." Jesus said to him, "No one who puts a hand to the plow and looks back is fit for the kingdom of God." (Luke 9:57–62)

INTRODUCTION

LET ME BEGIN THIS chapter by again reviewing the purpose of this book. I am drawing upon the history and present life of Church of the Crossroads in order to suggest ways in which churches of mainline Protestantism can respond faithfully and authentically to the process of their ongoing disestablishment in the North American context. I began with a chapter describing the establishment of Christendom in the fourth century and its subsequent disestablishment, a process that continues to influence the life of Christian churches. I related the establishment of Christendom to the ascendancy of a theology of glory, which has been the dominant theology of the Christian Church since the time of Constantine. I then contrasted this theology to a theology of the cross, which has the possibility of shaping the life, ministry and mission of churches who are willing to respond creatively and faithfully to the ongoing process of their disestablishment. In the second chapter, I introduced you more fully to the Church of the Crossroads by reviewing the important events and dimensions of its history, pointing out especially those times when it found itself on the edge of Hawaiʻi's social and political life. Now, in this chapter I want to turn to the present life and experience of this particular congregation and begin with an exploration of how it perceives its relationship to the world and how it attempts to carry out its Christian witness in the world.

Throughout, I am attempting to describe Church of the Crossroads as a congregation making its way, as faithfully as it can, towards a future expression of Christian community that will be bound not to a Christendom past with its theology of glory, nor to the North American cultural values of prestige, power and success, but that instead will have its life and ministry shaped by the cross of Jesus Christ and the leading of God's Spirit. Church of the Crossroads has recognized and is embracing the fact that, along with other churches of mainline Protestantism, it is being disestablished. I am writing this book not only in honor of this congregation of which I am the pastor, but also to invite other congregations who are being disestablished and moving towards the periphery of society to imagine the kind of faithful future for themselves that may become possible once this change in status is embraced. The fact that the mainline Protestant churches are being disestablished is not something to lament, but a change for which we can be thankful, for it can open our church communities up to new possibilities for faithfulness.

I want to suggest that a Christian community willing to journey towards such a faithful future will have a deep commitment to the world and its well-being. Such a commitment will not be an option but will be part and parcel of what it means to be a church. It will not be an option because a community risking the journey will understand God as the One who has an abiding compassion for the world and all of creation, a compassion that is most fully realized in the cross of Jesus Christ. In reflecting God's own commitment to the creation, the Christian community I have in mind will be marked by certain characteristics as it seeks to express in word and deed its own commitment to the well-being of the world.

First, it will do all it can to understand more deeply the *Zeitgeist*, the spirit of the time in which it lives. It will do so by listening to the world and the longings of its people so that it can respond in ways that will speak to those longings and also be faithful to the Gospel it professes. Secondly, such a community will have a dialectical relationship with the world that will make a genuine dialogue with the world possible. Thirdly, in a time such as the present, when society in its political and economic life acts in ways that are blatantly contrary to the spirit of the Gospel, the Christian community I have in mind will be led to take on a confessional stance as it seeks to speak to the world and act within it. Fourthly, it will have a concern not only for the well-being of humankind as it seeks to break down the barriers of hatred and oppression, which result in unmerited human suffering, but it will also have a deep abiding concern for the life of the planet itself. Finally, it will seek to engage in particular forms of ministry that bear the marks of humility, modesty, vulnerability, and risk of failure. These marks belong to a theology of the cross, and I will now describe how this theology is beginning to shape not only the communal life of Church of the Crossroads but also the way in which this community understands its engagement with the world.

THE CROSS AND GOD'S COMPASSION FOR THE WORLD

It is the evening of Good Friday at Church of the Crossroads. The choir has rehearsed its anthem and also the Taizé chants that will be an important part of the Good Friday Service, called simply "Prayers around the Cross." Of the three services organized for Holy Week, including the Maundy Thursday Service, the Good Friday Service, and the Saturday night Easter Vigil, this Good Friday Service is the best attended. It seems to speak not only to the spiritual needs of the members of the congregation but also to their deep concern for the world in which they live. The thoughts and prayers they bring to this service arise out of their own lives and also the needs of the world as they have come to know them. Prior to the service, the chairs (Crossroads is fortunate to have wooden chairs rather than pews) are arranged in a circular pattern so that people can see one another. Members of the choir are scattered among the others in the congregation. Dozens of votive candles provide much of the lighting. A rough wooden cross stands at the front of the chancel. It was placed there at the close of the Palm/Passion Sunday service following the reading of one of the passion narratives. That service ended in silence and this Good Friday Service begins in silence. Indeed, there will be periods of silence throughout the liturgy that is about to take place. The spoken words in this service are few in number.

After some opening chants sung by both choir and congregation, Psalm 22 is read and is then followed by a reading from the Gospel of John. Prayers for the world and for the church are offered. Then, after the singing of another chant or two and an anthem (the choir sings it from their places in the midst of the people), the cross is taken down from its stand and is placed in a horizontal position in the center of the circle. The worshipers are invited to come to the center, kneel at the cross if they wish, and bring their prayers for the places of suffering in the world that cry out for transformation, for the needs of those they know and love, and also for the deepest longings of their own lives. Many come forward as another chant is introduced. Others remain in their seats. After some time has passed, the congregation leaves the sanctuary in silence.

I have often asked myself why this service has become so important in the liturgical life of our congregation. There may be a number of reasons, some of which cannot be explained, but one reason is surely that the members of this particular congregation are open not only to their own longings and the needs of others in their faith community, but they are also deeply concerned about the suffering of the world, indeed of the whole creation. They understand that the God they worship is not aloof from the world but is present in its midst, most especially in its suffering. This they know, somehow, through the cross.

For them, the cross has become something more than the conventional sign that is associated with Christianity. The cross has become central in their understanding of the Christian faith. This understanding has not come easily because in their Christian pasts, if they had such a past, the cross was largely ignored and regarded simply as a stepping stone towards the glory and triumph of Easter, or perhaps it was used to proclaim the message that "Jesus died for your sins." For those gathered together at this Good Friday Service, a neglect of the cross is no longer acceptable. Also, the interpretation of the cross that was wrapped up totally, it seemed, in the message that Jesus died for your sins has become less and less meaningful. It's not that they no longer accept the reality of human sinfulness. They still know themselves as human beings who experience the separation from God, from one another and from the creation itself that comes from doing "those things we ought not to have done" and "leaving undone those things we ought to have done," and also the continuing need for forgiveness in their lives. At Church of the Crossroads, every Sunday service includes a corporate prayer of confession followed by an assurance of forgiveness. There used to be considerable discussion as to whether or not the service ought to include such a prayer, but this has now become an accepted and expected part of worship.

For Church of the Crossroads, the cross is beginning to take on a different meaning than the one given to it by Saint Anselm when he developed his substitution/satisfaction theory of the atonement. I will return to a discussion of this in the next chapter, but for now I want to say that one of the problems with Anselm's theory of the atonement is that it tends to keep God away from the suffering of the world and its people. That is what Anselm thought he must do. He felt he had to protect God from any involvement in suffering, either human or divine. Anselm simply could not conceive that an omnipotent, omniscient God could be subject to the kind of limitation that suffering implies. In Anselm's theory, then, God remains apart from the world and its suffering and looks on as Jesus submits to the cross and becomes the sufficient sacrifice for the sins of the world.

The members of Church of the Crossroads are beginning to see the cross not as an event that somehow makes satisfaction for the sins of the world, but more as a sign of God's own movement towards the world and its suffering. God is so committed to the well-being of the creation that God is willing to enter into those places that cry out for transformation. This movement of God towards the suffering of the world is rooted in God's compassion, God's capacity to "suffer with," which is the meaning of the word "compassion." The cross, then, is becoming for the people of Church of the Crossroads a sign that God is so committed to the world that God is willing to suffer with it and in it, and this in itself opens up the possibility of transformation, simply because it is *God* who is there, in the midst of the suffering. The new life of Easter is not something that simply arises *out* of the cross; rather, it is something inherent *in* it, not obviously present, perhaps, but latently present. That is why those who attend the Good Friday Service at Church of the Crossroads leave the sanctuary not in despair, but in hope. They are filled with hope not only for the well-being of their own lives but also for the well-being of the world in which they live.

LISTENING AND RESPONDING TO THE WORLD

The commitment of Church of the Crossroads to the well-being of the world has been articulated in a covenant adopted in March, 1992, as well as in a vision statement adopted in the year 2003 which I will discuss later. The 1992 covenant, known as the *Just Peace Covenant,* reads:

> *We, the Church of the Crossroads,*
> *in response to our belief in the love of God*
> *which unconditionally wills the good of all creation*
> *and our belief that aloha expressed as peace and justice,*
> *compassion and harmony,*

*is God's intention for all creation,
do hereby make covenant with God and with one another
to become a Just Peace Church
of the United Church of Christ.*

*We believe that although we are many members,
we are one body of Christ.
As a part of that body of Christ
we are called to love one another,
to do justice, to love kindness,
and to walk humbly with our God.*

*Responding to that call,
a goal of our ministry is by God's grace
to heal the brokenness
we experience in ourselves
and in our relationships with the creation,
with each other, and with God.*

*By the grace of God and the guidance of the Holy Spirit
we pledge ourselves as a community
to be a microcosm of the aloha
God intends for the world,
by living out in our life together
the integrity of creation, justice, and peace;
to seek the elimination of the causes of war
through nonviolent means;
to live towards the vision of a world
that is free from economic injustice,
oppression, racism, and sexism, and
to challenge the structures that perpetuate them;
to respect the human rights of persons
of all social and ethnic backgrounds,
physical and mental abilities,
gender, and sexual orientations;
to maintain aloha as a guiding force
for our ministry and mission.*

*Believing that this is God's world,
we pledge ourselves to carry out the vision
of the integrity of creation, justice and peace.*

Several features of this covenant are worthy of note. First, the covenant has been influenced greatly by the theme of "Peace, Justice, and the Integrity of Creation," which has been an ongoing theological and programmatic emphasis of the World Council of Churches for nearly two decades. Secondly, this covenant embraces an understanding of sin as relational in nature. In contrast to conventional Christianity's focus on sin as moral indiscretion, sin here is understood as the broken relationship we experience with God, with one another, and with the whole of creation. Therefore, the covenant envisions the work toward peace, justice, and the stewardship of creation as the healing of the "brokenness we experience in ourselves, and in our relationships with the creation, with each other, and with God." Finally, this covenant understands that the work of peace, justice and the integrity of creation is not only something *out there* to be enacted beyond the confines of the church. It is also something that has to be lived out *within the church.*

As an example of this "both/and" emphasis, I will mention the ongoing involvement of Church of the Crossroads in a faith-based community organization known as FACE (Faith Action for Community Equity). In recent years, this organization has been advocating passage of a living wage ordinance by the City and County of Honolulu and a fair living wage for hotel workers. Yet, how can the churches advocate such a policy in the larger community if they themselves do not pay a living wage to their own employees? The mission of the church in the world must also be lived out in the life of the churches themselves!

A covenant such as the *Just Peace Covenant of Church of the Crossroads* is impossible to fulfill unless the church first listens to the world. Therefore, it is vitally important to do all we can to understand the *Zeitgeist*, the spirit of the age in which we live. Church of the Crossroads attempts to listen to the world in a number of ways. Church members are encouraged to pay attention to the world as they carry out their vocational ministries in the world. There are informal reading groups organized around specific books and topics. The Sunday Morning Adult Education Hour often features series of discussions on important social issues and movements, such as justice and the global economy, civil rights, public education, health care, and the environmental crisis. The task always is to relate these issues to the Christian faith and the principles of Christian ethics. Furthermore, there are numerous community groups that sponsor talks and convocations in Weaver Hall, which serves not only as a social hall for the congregation but also as a community center. Members of the congregation are always informed about these talks and meetings, and many participate as a result.

In addition to these, a lectureship has been established at the church in memory of Yasu and Umematsu Watada, two members of the church who were important in its history. The overall theme of the lectures is "Peace, Justice, and the Environment." Thus far, five have come to serve as Watada lecturers: Daniel Alejandrez of *Barrios Unidos*, a community organization in Santa Cruz devoted to serving the needs of at-risk youth; Canon Naim Ateek of the Sabeel Ecumenical Institute located in Jerusalem, who informed the congregation of the plight of Palestinians in Israel/Palestine; the Rev. Adora Iris Lee, Minister for Environmental Justice with the Peace and Justice Ministries of the United Church of Christ; David Korten, author of *When Corporations Rule the World* and *The Great Turning: From Empire to Earth Community*, and well-known critic of the global economy; and Glenda Wildschut, a Commissioner on the Truth and Reconciliation Commission of South Africa. These are a number of ways through which the members of Church of the Crossroads do their best to listen to the world.

This leads to a question: How, then, do we describe the world in which we live? If I were to take the risk of generalization, I would have to say that the members of Church of the Crossroads have discovered the world as a place in which the struggle between hope and despair is the central defining issue. They would agree with Lieutenant-General Roméo Dallaire, the Canadian who led the UN Peacekeeping Mission in Rwanda, who in his book *Shake Hands with the Devil* describes in detail the failure of that mission to stop the genocide that took the lives of over eight hundred thousand Rwandans. Dallaire ends his book with these words:

> If September 11 taught us that we have to fight and win the "war on terrorism," it should also have taught us that if we do not immediately address the underlying (even if misguided) causes of those young terrorists' rage, we will not win the war. For every al-Qaeda bomber that we kill, there will be a thousand more volunteers from all over the earth to take his place. In the next decade, terrorists will acquire weapons of mass destruction. It is only a matter of time until a brilliant young chemist or smuggler obtains a nuclear, biological or chemical weapon and uses it to satisfy his very personal rage against us. Where does this rage come from? This book has demonstrated some of the causes. A heightened tribalism, the absence of human rights, economic collapses, brutal and corrupt military dictatorships, the AIDS pandemic, the effect of debt on nations, environmental degradation, overpopulation, poverty,

Engaging the World

hunger—the list goes on and on. Each of these and so many other reasons can lead directly to a people *having no hope for the future* (emphasis mine) and being forced in their poverty and despair to resort to violence just to survive. This lack of hope in the future is the root cause of rage. If we cannot provide hope for the untold masses of the world, then the future will be nothing but a repeat of Rwanda, Sierra Leone, the Congo and September 11.[1]

The members of Church of the Crossroads would largely support Dallaire's perspective. Interestingly, this same perspective is to be found in the concluding statement of the 2000 Campbell Seminar organized by Columbia Theological Seminary in Atlanta, Georgia. At this seminar, a number of distinguished theologians from throughout the world gathered together to discern what might be the mission of the church in our time and place. The concluding statement of the seminar, *Mission as Hope in Action*, identifies the Zeitgeist (spirit) of the age as one characterized by "negation, diminution, or dearth of hope."[2]

In the midst of the world's despair, the church's mission is indeed to put hope into action. First, however, the church must understand that the hope it professes is a *hope against hope*. In other words, the hope of the church must be distinguished from the false hope that is so tied to the culture's notions of optimism and progress. The witness of the church will represent a contrast to these notions, which are so embedded in popular culture, and will instead bear the marks of modesty, humility, and vulnerability. Christian hope arises out of a participation in Christ's passion and therefore must take into account the world as it really is. Such participation in the passion of Christ leads us to recognize the forces of death that are at work in the world and to question all notions of progress.[3]

This, then, is the mission of the church. It is to put hope into action and thus make room for the Gospel to faithfully address the despair of the world. Just as hope is to be distinguished from false hope, so is this newly shaped mission to be distinguished from the old notions of mission, which were so tied to ideologies of domination and the triumphalism of Christendom. Mission must now be envisioned as *missio dei*, God's mission. This is an understanding of mission that has become important for

1. Dallaire, *Shake Hands with the Devil*, 521–22.
2. Brueggemann, *Hope for the World*, 16.
3. For an excellent exploration of the notion of progress from an anthropological and historical perspective, see Wright, *A Short History of Progress*.

Church of the Crossroads as it seeks to engage the world. *Missio dei* recognizes that God's mission is larger than the church's mission. Christian mission is not first *Christian* mission, or the *church's* mission, but *God's* mission.[4] Walter Brueggemann comments:

> ... the church, with the important gains and sorry distortions of Christendom, must in the future practice its mission of "telling inside" and "enacting outside" with a due sense of humility. That humility is rooted in an awareness that distinguishes between its own mission as a gift of God and the mission of God that takes place not only in and through the church's mission but also before, outside, alongside the church's best obedience, and against the church when it is disobedient.[5]

Problematic to the carrying out of God's mission is whether or not the church can extricate itself enough from the world in order to truly engage it. In its Christendom past, the church was so deeply tied to its establishment status in the world that it was incapable of prophetically engaging the world. Another way to pose the question is to ask whether or not the church can separate itself from its own worldly status so that it can encounter the Jesus who calls it to discipleship. Richard Holloway puts it this way: "The paradox is that we have only heard of Jesus through an institution that has not experienced worldlessness for a very long time."[6]

The church's disengagement from the world is a most difficult task, not only because of our Christendom past, but because as an institution, the present-day church's financial underpinnings largely rely upon the benefits of the economic structures that themselves need to be addressed by the Gospel. This is an ongoing struggle for those who are members of Church of the Crossroads. How can our church in its action speak a word of hope to the world when at the same time the church relies upon the very economic structures that are causing such a lack of hope among the world's people? Furthermore, how can any church speak a prophetic word to political power when it enjoys a tax-exempt status within the society?

All of this is to say that the engagement of the church with the world will be marked not only by vulnerability, modesty, and humility, but also by considerable ambiguity. This ambiguity will be present in any

---

4. Brueggemann, *Hope for the World*, 7.
5. Ibid., 7–8.
6. Holloway, *Doubts and Loves*, 171.

community of faith when it understands that the process of disestablishment is an ongoing struggle. As much as we may critique a Christianity rooted in Christendom, our church communities continue to reflect the characteristics of established religion. However, once Christian communities envision a more faithful future, a future no longer bound to Christendom, they will begin to sense the ambiguities inherent in their present existence all the more, and they will have to learn to live with those ambiguities and begin to address them as well.

IN BUT NOT *OF* THE WORLD

Christian communities journeying to a more faithful future will need to articulate just how they are related to the world around them. Recently, I visited a congregation, and in the pew rack, I found a copy of its mission statement. It expressed a commitment "to grow as a congregation of the world." This upper-middle class and overwhelmingly Caucasian congregation in no way could be perceived as being a congregation *of* the world, and the understanding of their relationship with the world needed more attention. Apparently, this congregation had not taken the time to read the Gospel of John's rendition of the farewell prayer Jesus speaks on behalf of his disciples:

> ... I have given them your word, and the world has hated them because they do not belong to the world, just as I do not belong to the world. I am not asking you to take them out of the world, but I ask you to protect them from the evil one. They do not belong to the world, just as I do not belong to the world. Sanctify them in the truth; your word is truth. As you have sent me into the world, so I have sent them into the world. And for their sakes I sanctify myself, so that they may be sanctified in truth. (John 17:14–19)

The fact that we are not *of* the world has nothing to do with God's commitment to the well-being of the world. The Gospel of John is clear. God loves the world and so must we. "God so loved the world . . ." (John 3:14). Yet, it was this same world loved by God that did not know or accept the Christ. "He was in the world, and the world came into being through him, yet the world did not know him. He came to what was his own, and his own people did not accept him" (John 1:10–11).

Richard Holloway rightly points out that, in John's gospel, "world" does not mean "planet earth." Instead, the world in John's conception is "an organized structure of power and privilege that owes allegiance only to itself and even resists the approach of God."[7]

Consequently, if we take the risk of following the One who represents God in the world, we will be as aliens in the world. We will love the world as God loves the world, but we will not belong to it (John 17:16). Rather than belonging to the world, we belong to God and God's realm. God's realm is our true homeland. And yet we love the world and live in the world. It is all very strange. We find ourselves *in* the world (Jesus has sent us there!) but not *of* the world. A reverse way to put it is to say that we are not *of* the world, but most assuredly *in* it.

There is a dialectic between our faith and the world. From the standpoint of our faith, there is a contradiction between the world as we would want it to be and the world as it is. We would want the world "to be filled with the knowledge of God as the waters cover the sea" (Isa 11:9). Yet, that is not the way the world is. The world is filled with war and hatred, hunger and violence, cruelty and injustice.

If the world were to be what we want it to be, it would surely coincide with the life and ways of God's realm. In the words of the 65th chapter of Isaiah, it would be that place in which the sound of weeping would be no more, in which people would live out a lifetime, in which they would build houses and inhabit them, in which they would plant vineyards and eat their fruit. They would not build and another inhabit; they would not plant and another eat. They would not labor in vain, or bear children for calamity. And yes, the wolf and the lamb would feed together, the lion would eat straw like the ox, and none would hurt or destroy on all God's holy mountain.

I recall the time when Walter Brueggemann was a guest lecturer at Church of the Crossroads in 1998. I remember him standing before us, and in that unmistakable style of his, speaking the words of Isaiah chapter 65. Then he pointed to the main door of the sanctuary and said something like this: "Out there, they believe all this is nonsense, a utopian vision. But in here, we believe that these words constitute reality, our reality."

However, a caution needs to be noted. Liberal Protestant churches have often taken a visionary statement such as we find in Isaiah 65 and have tried to translate it into a social program. It has become a cliché in American churches embracing liberal Protestantism that "God has no

---

7. Ibid., 170.

hands but our hands." Religion has become something we *do*. It is as if the fulfillment of God's realm depends totally upon those of us who belong to the church. It is little wonder that there is so much frantic activity associated with the life of our churches! Church of the Crossroads has often been accused of just this. Underneath all of this activity and all of these good works, however, there is a misunderstanding as to how the churches are related to the world. If we are a church "of" the world, then the well-being of the world surely depends upon us.

If, however, we envision our relationship to the world as the gospel of John does, if we are to be "in" the world but not "of" the world, then our involvement in the world takes on the form of a faithful *witness* to the reality of God's realm, rather than an optimistic expectation that through us the promise of God's reign will be fulfilled. If the church were to see its work in the world in terms of witness rather than fulfillment, it would relieve the churches of the terrible burden of "saving the world." That is surely the work of God, which may, by God's grace, involve even us every now and then.

It is important to remember that the words we find in Isaiah 65 constitute an eschatological hope for the future. The vision articulated by the prophet Isaiah is a reality towards which we are journeying. Faithful acts that are accomplished along the way are only signs along the path and serve as an assurance for the Christian community that the realm of peace and wholeness is indeed what God intends for the whole of creation. This realm of justice and peace is the homeland to which we truly belong. As long as the world does not conform to the realm of peace and justice which we know as God's realm, we will find ourselves strangers to the world. We will be in the world, but not of the world.

At the same time that the liberal Protestant church in our time has been centered in an activism that places total responsibility for the world upon the actions of Christians, it has also failed to acknowledge the notion that Christians can do nothing apart from the costly grace of God. Although he lived in a different social and political context, Dietrich Bonhoeffer can be instructive. He had much to say about a worldly church that dispenses cheap grace:

> Cheap grace is the preaching of forgiveness without requiring repentance, baptism without church discipline, Communion without confession, absolution without personal confession. Cheap grace is grace without discipleship, grace without the cross, grace

without Jesus Christ, living and incarnate.... Such grace is *costly* because it calls us to follow and it is *grace* because it calls us to follow *Jesus Christ*.[8]

A church that dispenses cheap grace will have a difficult time disengaging from its surrounding culture to the extent that it may then engage the world with the truth of the Gospel. Furthermore, the Christian who relies upon the cheap grace dispensed by such a church will find himself or herself living comfortably in the world without having to pay any attention to the necessity of following Jesus Christ. Writes Bonhoeffer:

> If grace is God's answer, the gift of Christian life, then we cannot for a moment dispense with following Christ. But if grace is the data for my Christian life, it means that I set out to live the Christian life in the world with all my sins justified beforehand. I can go and sin as much as I like, and rely on this grace to forgive me, for after all the world is justified in principle by grace. I can therefore cling to my bourgeois secular existence, and remain as I was before, but with the added assurance that the grace of God will cover me. It is under the influence of this kind of "grace" that the world has been made "Christian," but at the cost of secularizing the Christian religion as never before. The antithesis between the Christian life and the life of bourgeois respectability is at an end. The Christian life comes to mean nothing more than living in the world and as the world, in being no different from the world, in fact, in being prohibited from being different from the world for the sake of grace.[9]

Christian communities, under the sign of the cross, will know that they are called to follow Jesus Christ, and that this commitment will set them apart from the world. At the same time they will enter the world bearing the cost of discipleship. They will know themselves to be *in* the world, surely, but not *of* the world.

CONFESSING THE FAITH

It is sobering to recall that Bonhoeffer wrote *The Cost of Discipleship* in Germany in 1937. Against the backdrop of a Protestant Church that was poised to acquiesce to the ideology and program of Hitler and the Third Reich, Bonhoeffer and others had come together in 1934 as the *Bekennende*

---

8. Bonhoeffer, *The Cost of Discipleship*, 44–45.
9. Ibid., 50–51.

Kirche or "confessing synod" of the German Protestant church and issued its Barmen Declaration. This Declaration was an act of *confession*. Without making a direct reference to Hitler and the Third Reich, through a series of both positive and negative statements, the Confessing Synod made it absolutely clear in the Barmen Declaration where it stood in relationship to its German context. The most famous article in the Barmen Declaration is the first.

> [We believe that] Jesus Christ, as he is attested for us in Holy Scripture, is the one Word of God which we have to hear and which we have to trust and obey in life and in death. . . .
>
> We *reject* the false doctrine, as though the Church could and would have to acknowledge as a source of its proclamation, apart from and besides this one Word of God, still other events and powers, figures and truths, as God's revelation.[10]

Most often, we view confession as an acknowledgment of wrongdoing, but it can also be a declaration of what Christians profess to be true *in the context of the world*. To confess is to own, avow, declare, reveal, or disclose what one considers to be true, not apart from the world, but within a specific worldly context. Therefore, as the members of the Confessing Church in Germany viewed with alarm the rise of the Third Reich, they were led to make their Barmen Declaration at a time when few regarded the program of the Nazi Party as a threat. They were concerned not with their own life and safety as a church, but with what they considered to be a *threat to the life of the world*.[11]

Confessions of faith within the context of the world are sometimes simple and straightforward and employ an economy of words. Sometimes, it need only be a single word or thought spoken with clarity. Such was the case in Germany in the 1930s when Heinrich Grüber, the founder of the Grüberbüro (an organization which helped pastors and Jews escape from the Nazis) said, simply, "The *gospel* in our time is that Jesus Christ was a Jew." The impact of this simple confession is brought into sharp relief when contrasted to a pronouncement that Ludwig Müller, Hitler's *Reichsbischof*, made about the same time. Müller, perhaps sensing some

---

10. A translation of the Barmen Declaration can be found in Cochrane, *The Church's Confession under Hitler*, 237ff.

11. Douglas John Hall regards anything that is a threat to the life of the world to be an occasion for the church to confess its faith. See Hall, *Confessing the Faith*, 11–12.

discomfort due to his endorsement of the ideology and program of the Third Reich, said, "I can accept *all* the creeds."[12] It is one thing to *profess* one's faith in all the creeds; it is another thing, and far more risky, to *confess* one's faith in a context in which life itself is being threatened by the "principalities and powers."

In the context of the American and Canadian political life of our day, the principalities and powers are being aided by political ideologies, the most notable of which is the neo-conservative ideology that now rules the actions of the US government. Just as in the case of the religious ideology embedded in the theology of glory, political ideology, as a tool of the empire, has the capacity to shape our reality. This point was brought home in a fine article by Ron Suskind published in the October 17, 2004 edition of the *New York Times Magazine*. Reporting a conversation he had with a senior advisor to President Bush, Suskind writes:

> The aide said that guys like me were "in what we call the reality-based community," which he defined as people who "believe that solutions emerge from your judicious study of discernible reality." I nodded and murmured something about enlightenment principles and empiricism. He cut me off. "That's not the way the world really works anymore," he continued. "We're an empire now, and when we act, we create our own reality. And while you're studying that reality—judiciously, as you will, we'll act again, creating other new realities, which you can study too, and that's how things will sort out. We're history's actors . . . and you, all of you, will be left to just study what we do."[13]

It is this kind of arrogance that led Jim Wallis of the Sojourners Community around the same time to propose to the Christian communities of the United States "a new confession of Christ." Alarmed by the ascendancy of a "theology of war," the language of "righteous empire," the use of talk of an American "mission" and "divine appointment" to "rid the world of evil," and a foreign policy that rejects the wisdom of international consultation, Jim Wallis formulated a confession based upon the pattern of the Barmen Declaration. A number of confessional stances, stated positively, are each followed by their antitheses. The first of these confessional stances and its antithesis reads as follows:

---

12. Heinrich Grüber's words and also those of Ludwig Müller are reported in Hall, *Confessing the Faith*, 84.

13. Suskind, "Without a Doubt," *New York Times Magazine*, October 17, 2004, 51.

> Jesus Christ, as attested in Holy Scripture, knows no national boundaries. Those who confess his name are found throughout the earth. Our allegiance to Christ takes priority over national identity. Whenever Christianity compromises with empire, the gospel of Christ is discredited.
>
> We reject the false teaching that any nation-state can ever be described with the words, "the light shines in the darkness and the darkness has not overcome it." These words, used in scripture, apply only to Christ. No political or religious leader has the right to twist them in the service of war.[14]

In the antithesis, Jim Wallis draws upon the speech in which President Bush referred to the United States as the "light that shines in the darkness."

I want to suggest that Christian communities wanting to journey towards a faithful future will be led to such acts of confession when they discern that in the world there is a threat to life itself, the life promised by Jesus in John's gospel, when he says, "I have come that they may have life and have it abundantly" (John 10:10). These acts of confession will be made even as these communities of faith acknowledge the ambiguities of their existence as churches of Christendom that are in the process of being disestablished.

The context in which the churches of the United States now find themselves has been described as a post-September 11th world. In such a world, filled as it is with a loss of civil liberties, a growing national deficit, a curtailment of programs assisting the poor, and the waging of a war against the people of Iraq, there is a need for Christian communities to confess the faith. Such confessions will be based on those parts of the church's professions of faith that have special bearing upon the context in which we now find ourselves.

At Church of the Crossroads, the Sunday sermon often becomes an act of confession. Preaching is taken seriously in this particular community of faith. Worshipers expect the preacher to disclose his or her own questions and struggles from the pulpit. They also expect the sermon to include a critical, historical approach to scripture. They not only anticipate that scripture will be taken seriously, but they also know that the worldly and human context in which they find themselves will enter the preaching. Although they expect the preacher to know the stories, the themes, the doctrines, and the great professions of faith of the Christian church,

---

14. Wallis, "A New Confession of Christ," October, 2004.

they trust that the preacher will not primarily be concerned with the need to profess the faith. Nor will they respond to preaching that separates the content of the faith from the human and worldly context in which life is lived. They most particularly respond when the preacher chooses to speak out of a sense of solidarity with them, taking into account their human experience and longings, both spoken and hidden. They want the preacher to have in mind his or her own experience and longings as well. They hope he or she will rely upon the One whom faith professes, rather than just the received truths of the tradition. They will appreciate it when he or she struggles to find the right words to say, and they know that when the right words are given, they may well turn out to be the old words of the church's tradition, but they will be spoken in a new way. For them, the act of preaching itself will have become more than a *professing the faith*; it will have become an act of *confessing the faith*.

A CONFESSIONAL SERMON

On occasion, a sermon that is preached at Church of the Crossroads is important enough to receive an even wider hearing as members send it to friends or as it is posted on the church's web site. I want to include one such sermon here. It is the sermon I preached on September 16, 2001, five days after the attack on the twin towers of the World Trade Center. The sermon, "Lamenting Our Losses," which is both pastoral and confessional, alludes to a number of themes and images: Jeremiah's lamentation over the city (Jer 1:1–4); the desire of God for a peaceful world (Ps 46); Jesus weeping over the city of Jerusalem (Luke 19:41–44); and especially towards the end of the sermon, Paul's instruction to the church in Rome to leave any kind of vengeance up to God (Rom 12:9–21). This idea that we human beings leave any kind of vengeance or retaliation up to God, stated at the beginning and at the end, becomes the main confessional stance of the sermon. This, then, is the sermon in its entirety.

> My sisters and brothers, as chilling as it was to witness those two airplanes crashing into the twin towers of the World Trade Center, and to hear of the airplanes crashing into the Pentagon and a wooded area in Pennsylvania, for us who are people of faith, it is equally chilling to hear all the easy speeches calling for revenge and retaliation. As a faith community and as a nation, we surely have to stop and take time to look deeply within ourselves in order

to find the wisdom that will enable us to move towards the peaceful world God desires for all her children.

Last Friday, when the sanctuary was open for prayer and reflection, one of the members of our church was seen there reading a portion of Thich Nhat Hanh's little book *Living Buddha, Living Christ*. Among the words she read are these: "There must be ways to solve our conflicts without killing. We must look at this. We have to find ways to help people get out of difficult situations, situations of conflict, without having to kill. Our collective wisdom and experience can be the torch lighting our path, showing us what to do. *Looking deeply together is the main task of a community or a church.*"[15]

My sisters and brothers, let us begin the task of looking deeply together. And let us begin just where we are. Let us begin with our grieving, our cries and laments spoken to one another and to God. Let us begin with our tears and our sorrow. If we stay there for a while, without immediately moving towards answers and solutions, we just may begin to receive the gift of wisdom from on high.

As a faith community we need to help our nation to lament, not just for a day, but for a while. For we also mourn. We mourn the death of brothers and sisters whose names we do not even know, but brothers and sisters nonetheless. As the bells tolled across the nation in remembrance of those who died, I was reminded of those well known words composed by John Donne over four hundred years ago when he heard the bells of St. Paul's Cathedral toll to announce the death of a human being whose name he did not know. He wrote: ". . . No man is an island, entire of itself; every man is a piece of the continent, a part of the main. If a clod be washed away by the sea, Europe is the less, as well as if a promontory were, as well as if a manor of thy friend's or of thine own were; any man's death diminishes me, because I am involved in mankind, and therefore never send to know for whom the bell tolls; it tolls for thee."[16]

And so we weep. We weep for ourselves. The deaths of our brothers and sisters are also our deaths. The deaths of those we did not even know have diminished us. Is this not why tears come to our eyes when we hear the stories of those who mourn the death of a wife, a husband, a child, a brother, a sister, a friend? Their loss is our loss. Therefore, we weep, we lament. We weep over the city, as did Jeremiah after the destruction of Jerusalem, as did Jesus when he entered Jerusalem five hundred years later.

15. Hanh, *Living Buddha, Living Christ*, 77.
16. Donne, *Devotions*, 108–9.

The loss of those whose lives were so shockingly and abruptly taken away is not the only loss we suffer, however. We have more losses to lament. There is the loss of our basic security, a security we have taken for granted. All of a sudden we find ourselves vulnerable, as vulnerable as the people of Europe during World War II, as vulnerable as the people of Hiroshima and Nagasaki, as vulnerable as the Jewish people during the dark days of the Holocaust, as vulnerable as Palestinians and the people of Iraq, as vulnerable as the Christians of the Sudan, as vulnerable as native peoples of every continent and nation. We are no longer secure, and we lament our loss, not only the loss of our security, but also the loss of our power. We, who could not prevent the deaths of five thousand people by a small group of terrorists armed with nothing more than knives and box cutters, are powerless. There is not a missile defense of any magnitude that could have prevented the events of last Tuesday. We are vulnerable and powerless, and so we lament. Perhaps, though, when we lament the loss of security and power, our lament is over something that was not real in the first place. Our lament may lead us to see a truth, that power and security (at least the kind we as a nation have relied upon) are illusions. The events of last Tuesday have unmasked these illusions, thanks be to God, for power and invulnerability are the illusions that have led us as a nation to run roughshod over the rest of humanity. Osama Bin Laden's hate has been fueled largely by our actions in the Persian Gulf War and our support of Israel at the expense of justice for the Palestinians.

We need to help our nation lament this loss of security and of power, for it is in lamenting this loss that our nation may be awakened to the wisdom that points to a new way of being in the world. If we are able to stay with our cries of despair, our vulnerability and loss of power, we may in truth be compelled to join the human race. We may begin to understand that if it is true for us as individual human beings, it is also true for us as a nation, that we are not an island unto ourselves, that we must begin to work for a world in which all, including the people of Afghanistan, will be considered as part of our own flesh, our own blood.

We seem surprised that so many people throughout the world have shed tears for us this past week, and well we should. For as a nation, by our wealth and our power, we have set ourselves apart and above others. And yet, others throughout the world know that we are part of them, and so they weep for us and for themselves. By the grace of God, lamenting our losses may lead us as a nation to ask the most piercing question of all: Why is that people hate us so much that they would be driven to do what they did? To continually ask ourselves that question may lead us finally to understand that the world will have no future if we do not come to terms with the inequalities created by our wealth and our greed, and the injustices created by our power. For it is these very inequalities and injustices that have led others to hate us and wish us harm. As a nation, we must indeed be guided by the vision of a world in which sharing by all will mean scarcity for none, a world in which no nation shall lift up sword against nation. In such a world, there will be no need for terrorists. In the absence of such a world, there will always be terrorism.

My sisters and brothers, the wisdom that may lead us and our nation towards a more peaceful and just world may indeed arise from our tears, our loss, our lament. For a while, we need to voice our lament, experience our loss, take time to weep, as did Jeremiah and Jesus. We need to look deeply together. Then, possibly, we may hear afresh additional words written by Thich Nhat Hanh: ". . . To preserve peace, our hearts must be at peace with the world, with our brothers and sisters. When we try to overcome evil with evil, we are not working for peace. If you say, 'Saddam Hussein is evil. We have to prevent him from continuing to be evil,' and if then you use the same means he has been using, you are exactly like him. Trying to overcome evil with evil is not the way to make peace."[17]

My brothers and sisters, the peaceful world for which we pray and hope itself does begin with a peaceful heart. To work for peace, we must have a peaceful heart. We must be at peace with one another. We must reach out to our Muslim brothers and sisters, and also our neighbors, in peace. We must examine our own lives so that we do not, by our privilege and wealth, contribute any more than humanly possible to the inequities of our present world. We must look to God for the wisdom that comes from on high. We must follow in the way of Jesus the Christ, whose way was the way of peace and justice. All of this may begin to happen if we find the grace and courage to lament, to grieve our losses, and to weep.

My inspiration this week came from a husband whose wife was on one of the airplanes that crashed into the World Trade Center. After telling his story, interrupted by his own tears and my tears, he was asked, "What do you think we should do?" He said simply and without hesitation, "We should let the criminal justice system look after those who were behind all of this," and then he went on to say something like this, "I do not believe in an eye for an eye and a tooth for a tooth. I do not want all of this to lead to the deaths of

---

17. Hanh, *Living Buddha, Living Christ*, 74–75.

more innocent women, men, and children. Let us allow the justice system which is already in place deal with this." Here was a human being who has a peaceful heart, who has allowed himself to lament well and voice his cry unto God who is a God of compassion and comfort, the God of peace. Here is a human being ready to leave vengeance up to God, a human being ready to overcome evil with good. May his wounded and wise spirit be in us, and in the leaders and people of our nation. So help us, God.

WORD AND DEED

I have included the entire text of this sermon because I want to make the point that as the church engages the world, the spoken confession of faith cannot be neglected. So often, in the liberal mainline church, we hear repeated over and over again the popular idea that talk is cheap and that it is "walking the walk" that is important. I would like to make a correction to that popular notion. For Christian communities who are being disestablished and who are discovering a new relationship to the world, which we have described as being in the world but not of the world, the spoken word as well as acts that are done in the world will serve to engage that same world. When a sermon is preached, the world, represented by the curious folk who stay at the edge of the worshiping community, is, in a sense, "listening in" as the faith is being professed and perhaps, even more importantly in a time such as ours, confessed.

Preaching and teaching are valued at Church of the Crossroads, and action as well. The vision statement of the Church of the Crossroads adopted in January of 2003 as part of its *New Creation Initiative* attempts to state what the church intends to be and do. This statement is the result of a four-year discernment process carried out under the guidance of the Center for Parish Development. The statement reads as follows:

> Church of the Crossroads, a community of faith rooted in the life, faith, and ministry of Jesus Christ and committed to personal and social transformation and the stewardship of the earth, seeks to embody the three-fold missional activity of God: (1) the mission of nurture; (2) the mission of service; and (3) the mission of peace with justice, and the stewardship of the earth.

In the next chapter, I will turn to the mission of nurture as I speak of personal well-being within the community of faith. Here, I want to speak of

Engaging the World

the way the congregation envisions the mission of service and the mission of peace with justice, and the stewardship of the earth. The congregation recognizes the need to care for the needs of the hungry and homeless, even though it knows that it falls far short of the task. The congregation also understands that the needs of the earth, the ʻaina itself, need also to be served, especially in our time when we have become so aware of the threat of global warming. In its mission of service, the congregation wants to be guided by the practice of hospitality and the goal of friendship, and the spirit of solidarity. It realizes that service can easily become another form of domination when those with power serve those without power, and so it wants to understand that service in a Gospel context always bears a measure of reciprocity and mutuality. Finally, Church of the Crossroads wants to understand that if its service is carried out faithfully, it will also be led to a *public* witness on behalf of peace, justice and the stewardship of creation that will bring it into an engagement with the political process.

Underneath all this, there is an understanding of mission as God's mission, *missio dei*. In order for God to carry out God's own mission, God does not need the church. That is a humbling thought. God's presence and activity in the world are larger and broader than the church. Yet, it is the task of the church to conform itself to God's mission, and when it fails to do so, it will find itself under divine judgment.

The difficulty arises when the church seeks to put a vision "written large" into particular, concrete action. The vision statement above, which has become known as the New Creation Initiative has indeed resulted in some modest actions. Among these, I would point to the participation of the church in peace marches and gatherings opposing the war on Iraq and the church's role in founding the Hawaiʻi Friends of Sabeel, a chapter of the Sabeel Ecumenical Institute located in Jerusalem which is committed to security for Israelis and justice for Palestinians. On a local level, the church has participated in the work of Faith Action for Community Equity (FACE), an interfaith community organization based on the Alinsky model, which does indeed act, often successfully, on specific issues of transportation, safety, housing, health care, and living wage. The church has also joined other congregations, religious communities, and a synagogue in Family Promise of Hawaiʻi, a program in which homeless families are housed on a rotating basis in church and temple buildings. Church of the Crossroads has publicly supported same-sex marriage and the civil rights of gays and lesbians within the society. Its involvements on behalf of the earth itself include restoration work in the area of the ancient *Ulupo Heiau* under the leadership of Chuck Burrows, a church member, and more recently, involvement in witness and action around global warming and issues of sustainability.

A MODEST WITNESS

The word "modest" should be underscored in all of the efforts mentioned above. The church, aware of its Christendom underpinnings and also of the process of disestablishment, needs to rid itself of any illusions of success and achievement when it comes to mission. Its witness and service will necessarily be modest in face of the eschatological hope it places in God's promise of the whole creation transformed and made new.

It must also be ready to experience vulnerability as it seeks to engage the world in its witness, and not only vulnerability, but also failure. At Church of the Crossroads, we will never forget one such instance of failure. Nearly four years ago, the church once again had to face a phenomenon that has occurred over and over again in its more recent past. Because of the open and freely accessible church grounds and the more benign climate of Hawai'i, homeless people have tended to settle in for the night on the church grounds. Four years ago, the number of homeless men and women sleeping at the church grew to over forty persons. Generally, as it has become aware of the resident homeless, "the homeless at the doorstep" as I put it, the church community has had an informal policy of benign neglect. In other words, the church has known that the homeless sleep on the church grounds, but in recent years it has not seen fit to be involved in the situation.

Four years ago, a homeless man appeared in the church office. He was badly bruised and bandaged. He said that violence had broken out among the homeless the night before and that he had ended up in the emergency room. This was not the first violent incident that had taken place. Then, I looked out my window and witnessed a man actually measuring the length of one of the old pews located around the courtyard, provided as places for people to sit during the day. The man then began to cut a blanket so that it would fit the length of the pew. Something in me said that we were headed for more and more trouble. Therefore, rather reluctantly, I made a unilateral decision (in retrospect, I probably should have consulted others). I announced that there would be a moratorium placed on the homeless sleeping at the church until we could decide what kind of church involvement in the situation might be possible.

The homeless, for the time being, were not allowed to sleep at the church. Christmas Eve arrived and the midnight service of lessons and carols. I usually give a sermon as part of the service. On this particular Christmas Eve, the entire chancel had been blocked off because of all the structural repairs that were then taking place. In my Christmas Eve sermon, I used this unsightly appearance of the chancel as a way to describe the story of the infant Jesus being born in a barn suitable for animals and laid in a feeding trough, and as a sign that God had come to dwell among the poor of the earth. All of a sudden, my sermon was interrupted by a man screaming obscenities against the church out in the courtyard. In no uncertain terms, he was protesting the decision to remove the homeless from the church grounds. In a moment of insight (or perhaps bewilderment), I stopped preaching and allowed the man to complete his word of judgment against the church. Then I said something like this: "Now we can see how very difficult it is to put the truth of the incarnation, God's coming to be with the poor and lowly of the earth, into action."

This whole event prompted the church to engage in what churches usually do in this kind of situation—a study. An elaborate proposal for the church's presence among the homeless on a nightly basis was drawn up as a result of the study and approved by the congregation. The only problem with it is that it turned out to be a financially prohibitive proposal, and so the whole plan was dropped. Even though Church of the Crossroads is now housing homeless families for just one week every three months through Family Promise of Hawai'i, at that time the church experienced a deep failure in its effort to embody *missio dei,* God's mission. Yet, the church also gained wisdom in the process. It began to understand that as a church trying to make its way from a Christendom past, under which it still labors, into an awkward present and then perhaps on to a more faithful future, it must have no illusions about its own adequacy, its faithfulness, and its ability to carry out the mission with which it has been entrusted. Indeed, it must be ready, even when it engages the world in modest ways, to know the vulnerability that comes with costly discipleship and also its failure to be the church God calls it to be.

4

Our Stories at the Foot of the Cross

I came here in '61 and I visited a whole lot of ethnic churches. At each one of them, as I left after the close of the service, I was patted on the shoulder and told that I would probably be much happier at a "haole" (Caucasian) church. And so I went to a "haole" church for a year, and I was not happy there. Finally, I came over here one Sunday, and I remember, so distinctly, Fred Buren and his wife were sitting in front of me. They were in the "hippie" category that day. They had ragged clothes and dirty feet and no shoes . . . the whole works. I sat there looking at them and I said to myself, "If this church is that accepting of whoever walks in the door, then this is where I belong," and so I joined.

—Judy Rantala

I think the way we support one another in this community is exceptional. I myself have felt supported. My husband is going through some medical challenges as he ages, and I could name a half dozen people that I can call, just from Church of the Crossroads. We've been in Hawai'i for twenty years, so I have lots of friends. But, I feel so supported by the people in this congregation. That's a big thing, and I think that there is not only a lot of mutual support within the congregation, I also think the congregation reaches out and supports a lot of good things beyond the church doors.

—Mary Reese

I was raised in a Congregational church, but I left when I went to college and became a humanities major, and it took me fifty years to get back, but after my daughter was murdered, I found I needed to find a place of solace, and so I belonged to a few places, including a "New Thought" church for a few years which didn't give me much, and then I came to Crossroads when Neal was leading a prayer vigil before the same-sex marriage vote, and I was so impressed with the good feelings that I started coming. And so I'm happy to be here, although I am still searching. I've found solace here, and I think people accept me even though I may not be a full-time believer, but I'm still looking, waiting for the epiphany.

—Mona Altiery

... God has so arranged the body, giving greater honor to the inferior member that there may be no dissension within the body, but the members have the same care for one another. If one member suffers, all suffer together with it; if one member is honored, all rejoice together with it. (1 Cor 12:24b–26)

THE WORLD AND PERSONAL WHOLENESS

THE READER WILL RECALL that following my review of the history of Church of the Crossroads, I turned to the present life of the congregation and began by describing its relationship to and its engagement of the world. Only now do I write on the theme of personal well-being within the community of faith. I have intentionally ordered the subjects. Usually, when people write about church communities, they begin with the well-being of the members of the church and then turn to the church's involvement in the world. The problem has been, however, that many congregations have so concentrated on the individual needs of their members that they never get around to a faithful witness in the world. That is why I intentionally began with the theme of the church's involvement in the world, and now will turn to the more personal, pastoral dimensions of our life together within our community of faith. Both the "outer" and "inner" dimensions of the life of a congregation need to be considered as it chooses to extricate itself from both the trappings of its Christendom past and the continuing influence that same Christendom exerts upon its present life, while it embarks on a journey towards a more faithful expression of the Christian movement.

At Church of the Crossroads, we continue to struggle for a balance between our concern for the world and our care for one another, between these outer and inner dimensions. This struggle, I believe, has arisen from our history as a congregation. Following the bold witness of the congregation in the midst of the Vietnam War, there was a growing realization within the community that insufficient attention had been paid to the feelings and concerns of those members of the church who could not agree with the church's act of giving sanctuary to the servicemen who were AWOL. It took some time before this growing realization could be articulated clearly.

Even following the Sanctuary event, those who remained in the church did not sense the need to give much priority to the care of one another. The church did not even see fit to call a pastor. Instead, a Coordinator of Ministries was called to serve the church. Now, in retrospect, members of Crossroads who were involved in the Sanctuary event realize that a pastor was what the church really needed at the time. Today, in the congregation, there is a commitment both to care for one another within the church community and, at the same time, to engage in a witness for peace and justice and the integrity of creation in the world.

Actually, there is a connection between the well-being of individual persons and the well-being of the world. That connection was articulated by the 2000 Campbell Seminar in the document it produced, "Mission as Hope in Action." The same struggle between hope and despair encountered in the world will also be found in the lives of individual human beings, not only in those who are poor, but in those who are of the middle class. The Campbell Seminar spoke of the "hidden despair of those who have and the open despair of those who do not."[1] Most problematic for the mainline Protestant congregation is the hidden despair of the affluent. Said the members of the Campbell Seminar, "The greatest test of the Christian message in our time is whether it is able to engage and transform that despair."[2] The hidden despair among the affluent is evidenced in the symptomatic attitudes with which we are all familiar: a sense of futility when it comes to the church's social and political witness; a growing apathy in the face of the world's ills; a retreat into individual spirituality; a desperate attempt to keep up appearances; and, at times, a boredom, an *ennui* that arises out of a feeling of emptiness and purposelessness.

Until a community of faith pays attention to the hidden despair present among its members, there can never be a real sense of solidarity with

---

1. Brueggemann, *Hope for the World*, 16.
2. Ibid.

those in the world who are open about their despair. If the members of a church community do not address their own despair, they will inevitably approach the poor of the world with a paternalistic attitude, rather than in a spirit of compassion.

SPEAKING OUR DESPAIR

It is the Fall of the year 2002, and members of Church of the Crossroads have gathered in the Ross-Davis Meeting Room for the first Adult Education session since the close of summer. The series has been named *Sharing our Faith Journeys*. A number of people, one person per session, have been chosen to speak of their lives and their journeys. They have been asked to describe the personal and world events that have shaped them, the questions and struggles that have commanded their attention, as well as the faith that has sustained them. Their presentations are not scrutinized beforehand. They are given the freedom to say whatever they wish. In each session, lasting an hour, time is given for response and conversation among those who have gathered to listen.

Each session turns out to be a remarkable occasion. The attendance grows so that by the end of the series, more sessions have to be added because others have stepped forward to offer their stories. Extra chairs have to be transported from the social hall to the meeting room. The presentations are sprinkled with both pathos and humor. On one Sunday, a teacher of geography, in his late forties, speaks of his growing-up years, his relationships, including his failed marriages, his faith, and most poignantly, his struggle with a benign brain tumor that has left him physically challenged and legally blind. His humor is disarming. On another Sunday, a retired woman speaks of her childhood in a plantation village on the island of Kauaʻi, her struggle to make sense of her mother's faith and piety, her marriage into a Hawaiian family, her relationship with her husband with all its ups and downs, and the way in which Church of the Crossroads has given her the "space" both to express her continuing doubts about the claims of the Christian faith and, at the same time, to grow as a human being. On another occasion, a gay middle-aged man speaks of his past and present relationship to the church, his ongoing struggle to appreciate the God of the Hebrew and Christian scriptures, and the experience he has had bringing up two adopted Cambodian boys as a single parent. In another session, a middle-aged man shares the lifelong struggle he has had with acute diabetes and a severe mental disorder, and also his abiding faith. The previous Sunday, his wife humorously spoke of her experience growing up Catholic in Philadelphia and her journey into liberal Protestantism. Still another, a Native Hawaiian, shares his indigenous roots, his struggle to relate his inherited Hawaiian spirituality to the Christian faith, and his lifelong commitment to the integrity of creation. All of these sessions open others up to their own life experiences. A genuine sense of community is thereby created.

Even more poignant stories are shared in other gatherings, both informal and formal. There is the story of the mother whose child was murdered and whose body was never found. There is the story of the older woman who, when she was young, became pregnant and gave up her son for adoption. Because of periods of deep clinical depression, she never disclosed this truth of her life to anyone until she was led to do so in the context of counseling at an interfaith counseling center, which in turn set her free to tell her story in her faith community. I am thinking also of the mother who faced a life-threatening situation after being stabbed repeatedly by her son who was, at the time, under the influence of drugs. There is the story of the gay man who, for a number of years, cared for a partner who had become severely mentally ill and also the story of the man who lives courageously with AIDS. Then, there is the story of the young married woman whose husband finally acted on his own awareness of his true gender identity and began living as a woman. I have in mind also the story of the brilliant lawyer, at times unemployed or underemployed, who struggles on a daily basis with her mental illness.

Our faith community, with all of its faults and failures, not to mention its awkwardness in this time of transition as it embraces the ongoing process of its disestablishment in the world, is a remarkable community of faith in many ways. I would describe it as a community in which its members have discovered a remarkable freedom to acknowledge the reality of despair in their lives and the courage to speak about it openly. Søren Kierkegaard, more than a century ago, spoke of this kind of deep despair as a sickness unto death. He described it as a despair that "does not even know that it is despair."[3] At Church of the Crossroads, we are learning to speak this kind of despair. Later, I will attempt to describe some of the factors that have contributed to a spirit of openness in the congregation.

---

3. Kierkegaard, *The Sickness unto Death*, 42.

For now, I will simply say that this community has become a place where despair can be named and spoken.

At times, as we have seen, this despair that does not know itself to be despair is spoken out of one's own human experience. At times, the despair is named as members speak of their experience in the world: their encounters with the poor and homeless in the midst of their own affluence; the despair they deeply feel over the unjustified war on Iraq; and their fears and uncertainty about the world their children and grandchildren will inherit. As all this despair is named and spoken, a remarkable thing begins to happen. The despair is received and honored by the community, and, by the grace of God, seeds of hope are planted. In the naming of our despair, we somehow are brought closer to that which is longed for but not seen, the subject matter of hope. In the context of a faith community, both the experience of despair and the affirmation of hope can be acknowledged, openly and honestly, not only by the individual member of the church but also by those surrounding him or her. Wrote St. Paul to the Church in Corinth, "If one member suffers, all suffer together with it; if one member is honored, all rejoice together with it" (1 Cor 12:26).

THE WORK OF JESUS THE CHRIST

You will notice that I have not said anything about guilt. I have come to understand that despair rather than guilt is at the heart of the anxiety of modernity and now post-modernity. Paul Tillich, in *The Courage to Be*, offers an instructive analysis of anxiety. He names three types of anxiety: the anxiety of fate and death, the anxiety of guilt and condemnation, and the anxiety of meaninglessness and despair. All of these anxieties, he says, belong to the human condition in every time and place. However, each of these anxieties gains prominence in particular periods of human history. In the ancient Mediterranean world in which the Christian movement first tried to make its way, it was the problem of fate and death that occupied human beings; in the Middle Ages, it was the problem of guilt and condemnation; and in the modern period, it is the problem of meaninglessness and despair that besets human beings.

Christian communities willing to embrace their own disestablishment in the world will be willing to address this anxiety of meaninglessness and despair, simply because they will have been set free themselves from the official optimism of popular culture, an optimism that has been incapable of making room for any feelings of hopelessness. Such communities will truly be a gift to those who belong to our society, for they will be able to engage human beings at the deepest levels of their experience.

As for the anxiety associated with fate and death, it will always be with us, as well as the anxiety of guilt and condemnation. But despair combined with meaninglessness is the overwhelming anxiety of our lives. Yet, the church, caught up in its Christendom past, continues to focus on the anxiety of guilt and condemnation as if this were the only anxiety that really matters. Whether the focus on guilt is just a way to avoid the deeper human issues of the day, or whether this focus is simply a matter of habit, churches have seemed reluctant to confront the issue of hidden despair.

Douglas John Hall, in *Professing the Faith*, correlates each of the anxieties named by Paul Tillich to a corresponding theory of the atonement.[4] Thus, the anxiety of fate and death, prominent in the classical period of Christian theology, is answered by the *ransom theory* of the atonement. In this theory, the human condition is one of oppression. Humanity, enslaved tragically to the demonic, to the principalities and powers, is rescued from its predicament by Jesus the deliverer, the liberator. The image projected by this theory is "Christ the Victor" who conquers the forces of evil, thereby setting free those with whom he has identified himself.

The anxiety of guilt and condemnation is answered by the *substitution theory* of the atonement, articulated in the eleventh century by Anselm of Canterbury. Here, human beings are viewed as fallen creatures, caught in a web of guilt and condemnation. In this theory, Christ is a sacrificial victim who is substituted for a humankind that deserves to die because of its sinfulness. Christ, perfectly innocent and without sin, is substituted for us and pays the price of death upon the cross, thereby freeing us from our guilt.

The third atonement theology Hall describes is characterized by the idea of *demonstration* or *revelation*. This theory, in part, correlates to the modern anxiety of meaninglessness and despair. The theory is associated with Peter Abelard (1079–1142) but it came into its own when it was adopted by liberal Protestantism. Here, human beings are characterized by ignorance, not a mere lack of knowledge, but the ignorance of being loved by the Eternal, of being a beloved creature. For human beings, this is truly a pathetic condition. In Abelard's thinking, as in Anselm's, the

---

4. See Hall, *Professing the Faith*, 413–39.

cross speaks of sacrifice, but in Abelard the intention of the sacrifice is not to make amends, but to reveal God's mercy and grace. As we become hearers of the gospel through the testimony of the church, we find ourselves moved by God's love and forgiveness demonstrated by Jesus on the cross, with the result that we become new, beloved creatures in Christ.

There are difficulties associated with each of these atonement theories. Here, I mention only the difficulties that arise when we human beings are brought into the picture. In the first two theories, the ransom and the substitution theories of the atonement, we human beings are left out of the equation. Everything is done for us apart from our own participation in the work of Jesus. It is therefore difficult for us to feel our connection with the Jesus who frees us from our oppression or who substitutes himself for our sin. His work is carried out whether or not we are involved.

In the demonstration/revelation theory of the atonement, the opposite is true. We human beings are *too* subjectively involved. The work of Jesus on the cross has no objective reality apart from our acceptance of God's love and forgiveness as demonstrated in the cross. If this is the case, the reality of God's prevenient grace, which does not depend upon human awareness or participation, cannot be recognized. Somehow, a way of speaking of the atonement must be found that will both keep the objective reality of the cross in place and, at the same time, connect us as human beings to that reality.

THE HUMAN JESUS

Once the members of Church of the Crossroads have spoken their despair, once their despair has been received and honored by the members of their faith community, they often express a desire to relate their human experience to the Christian faith. More particularly, they seek to relate their lives to the Jesus who is at the center of Christian faith. They are at first not so interested in a Christ of glory but rather seek a human Jesus. They seek a Jesus with whom they can identify.

This is not easily accomplished, simply because Christendom has been far more interested in the Christ of glory than in the human Jesus of the gospels. Because a focus on the human Jesus has been neglected by the churches of Christendom, it will not be easy for contemporary Christians to discover the human Jesus with whom they can identify. One of the values of the demonstration/revelation theory of the atonement is that it does restore this needed emphasis on the human Jesus. This theory of the atonement draws our attention to the humanity of Jesus and calls upon us to identify with this human being, much like us, who on the cross demonstrates the love, mercy, and forgiveness of God. At the same time, besides the problem that the efficacy of the cross is too dependent upon our subjective human response, there are additional problems that arise with this theory. One difficulty may be characterized as psychological. Human beings are called to accept the unconditional love of God shown in the cross, but psychologists teach us that love is never easily received and appropriated. We may admire the love demonstrated by the one who "lays down his life for his friends," but more often than not, we reject that kind of love when it is presented to us, for it represents "an invasion of the self and a terrible judgment of the self's bid for autonomy."[5]

Another, more serious, problem arises with liberal Protestantism's later development of this theory of the atonement. In liberal Protestantism's hands, the human Jesus of Peter Abelard became the *Truly Human Jesus*, a Jesus whose humanity was so perfect that he still remains out of reach for human beings such as us. Writes Douglas John Hall,

> The problem was, I think, that Jesus for liberalism became a model of humanity so perfect, so absolute in every virtue, so blameless in respect to every sin recognized by his Victorian and other champions, that in the long run the very humanity of the liberal Jesus functioned in much the same way as did the divinity of the conservative Jesus—that is, to distinguish him conspicuously from the rest of us.[6]

What is needed is a human Jesus who knows our existential despair, a human Jesus with whom we can identify.

JESUS THE REPRESENTATIVE

In the meanwhile, conservative and conventional Christian churches have continued to focus on guilt and condemnation as if these were the only problems that really matter. Certainly, for human beings in every age the anxiety of guilt and condemnation is a problem. There is still a lot of guilt to be found in human beings. Perhaps, however, we ought to find a way of speaking about guilt without immediately resorting to Anselm

---

5. Ibid., 467.
6. Ibid., 457.

for answers. Rather than laying all of our guilt on Jesus and viewing God as the righteous condemner of our guilt, we perhaps might begin to see God as taking our guilt into God's own self. After all, guilt arises when we commit an offense, and God has granted us the freedom to "not do what I want" but "do the very thing that I hate" (Romans 7:15). How could God create us as free human beings and then expect us to remain guiltless? If God, then, is somehow responsible for our guilt, is it not then possible to imagine God absorbing that guilt into God's own being?

The almost exclusive focus that the church places on the anxiety of guilt and condemnation is evident in the hymns the church sings and the language the church speaks. Both continue to reflect the church's focus on the problem of human sinfulness. Guilt and condemnation often make their way into sermons that identify sinfulness not as one's separation from God or neighbor, but as the committing of moral indiscretions of one kind or other. The sermons then proceed to provide the answer that "Jesus died for your sins." The sermon might then be followed by a hymn such as *How Great Thou Art*, the third stanza of which reads:

> And when I think, that God, His Son not sparing,
> Sent Him to die, I scarce can take it in;
> That on the Cross, my burden gladly bearing,
> He bled and died to take away my sin.[7]

Such a focus on guilt leads us to define sin too narrowly. Sin is surely more than the moral indiscretions that lead us to feel guilty. Sin is a relational term. It has to do with our broken relationship with God, with one another, and with the earth itself. At times, this separation comes about because of what we do. Most often, however, the separation arises from an underlying desire for human autonomy which sets us apart from others and "The Other." In its relational sense, sin can be described in both individual and corporate ways. In an individual sense, sin can be spoken of in terms of broken personal relationships. In its corporate sense, it may be described as the economic injustice, violence, and warfare that fracture our relationship to the earth and its people. It is the breaking of these relationships, whether in an individual or a corporate sense, that results

---

7. Carl Gustav Boberg wrote the hymn in 1885. It was first published in 1886. The 3rd stanza was written and added to the hymn by Stuart K. Hine, © 1953, renewed 1981 Manna Music, Inc., used by permission.

in a state of alienation, and that, in turn can create within us the anxiety of despair and meaninglessness. Barbara Brown Taylor writes:

> In a postmodern age, the language of sin and salvation will only communicate with the disillusioned if it is absolutely truthful about the realities of their lives, and if it supports them to name those realities for themselves. The days are long gone when most preachers can stand up in pulpits and name people's sins for them. They do not have that authority anymore. What they can do, I believe, is to describe the experience of sin and its aftermath so vividly that people can identify its presence in their own lives, not as a chronic source of guilt, nor as sure proof that they are inherently bad, but as the part of their individual and corporate lives that is crying out for change.[8]

The church, it seems, is still caught up in the notion that sin is first and foremost moral indiscretion. This understanding of sin lies in the background of Anselm's substitution theory of the atonement. There is a seeming reluctance in the church to explore the problems associated with this theory, which has been the dominant interpretation of the priestly work of Jesus for the past thousand years. We have already noted that this theory fails to make a connection between Jesus and our humanity.

In the last chapter, I noted that another problem with this theory is that it keeps God away from the suffering of Jesus and therefore the suffering of the world. Anselm needed to do that, because for him, it was impossible to conceive of a God who suffers. God must be kept away from any kind of suffering. It was and is still believed that if God suffers in any way, God's own power is compromised. God's power must not be weakened by suffering. In the conventional understanding of Christians, God becomes a God who is up there and out there, all powerful, who watches at a distance while the sinless, pure Son goes to the cross to make satisfaction for the sins of humankind. The problem is that if we human beings seek to safeguard God's power by not allowing God to suffer, if we keep God apart from the suffering of Jesus, then God becomes remote and separate from us also.

Dietrich Bonhoeffer, who went to prison and his death because of his opposition to Adolph Hitler, once wrote that "Man's religiosity makes him look in his distress to the power of God in the world . . . the Bible

---

8. Taylor, *Speaking of Sin*, 29.

directs man to God's powerlessness and suffering." Then, from the depths of his own suffering, he added "Only a suffering God can help."[9]

I believe that one of the most important contributions Douglas John Hall has made to the church is his articulation of a contrasting interpretation of the work that Jesus accomplished through the cross. Briefly, Hall, along with other contemporary theologians including Dorothee Sölle (in her book *Suffering*), and Hendrikus Berkhof, employs the metaphor of "representation." On the cross, Jesus represents the God who, in compassion, approaches human beings, desiring for them and for the whole creation a newness of life. Jesus also represents those same human beings caught up in meaningless despair who, in hope and perhaps anger, stand before God while longing for that same newness of life and the presence of God in their lives. In the cross, God moves towards humankind and humankind moves towards God. God and humankind meet in Jesus the Representative. In representing the God who in compassion suffers with and on behalf of humankind, Jesus himself suffers, and in representing humankind, Jesus angrily cries out aloud in existential despair, "My God, my God, why have you forsaken me?" (Mark 14:34). For us, this cry becomes the most important word Jesus speaks from the cross, for it not only embraces the hidden despair of our lives that finally dares to be named and spoken, but it also embraces our longing and the longing of the world for God, in whose presence there is hope and the promise of newness of life.

This profound notion of representation has the possibility of helping the church rethink the way it has understood the death of Jesus on the cross as it relates to our existential situation. The idea of Jesus as representative is already making its way into the hymnology of the church. I might suggest that when hymn writers incorporate a new theological understanding in their hymns, we can take heart that theological renewal may indeed emerge in the church, simply because the hymns of the church are often the last aspects of worship to undergo change. The following hymn written by Brian Wren employs the idea of representation. It may be sung to the tune *Passion Chorale*.

---

9. Bonhoeffer, *Letters and Papers from Prison: The Enlarged Edition*, 361.

Here hangs a man discarded,
a scarecrow hosted high,
a nonsense pointing nowhere
to all who hurry by.

Can such a clown of sorrows
still bring a useful word
where faith and love seem phantoms
and every hope absurd?

Yet here is help and comfort
to lives by comfort bound
when drums of dazzling progress
give strangely hollow sound;

Life emptied of all meaning,
drained out in bleak distress,
can share in broken silence
our deepest emptiness;

And love that freely entered
the pit of life's despair
can name our hidden darkness
and suffer with us there.

Lord, if you now are risen,
help all who long for light
to hold the hand of promise
till faith receives its sight.[10]

The words of this hymn reveal the connection between the human Jesus on the cross and the human being who also cries out in existential despair. In this understanding of the priestly work of Jesus, though, the connection is not just between the human Jesus and us. Because the metaphor of the representative also includes the notion that the one representing us also represents another reality (for example, the person elected to Congress represents both his or her constituency and also the decisions of government itself), there is a transcendent dimension in the idea of Jesus as representative. Because Jesus on the cross also represents God, Jesus cannot be completely limited to that which is human. By maintaining a transcendent dimension within the person of Jesus, this way of describing the work of Jesus addresses one of the problems associated

---

10. Wren, "Here Hangs a Man Discarded," Words © 1975, 1995 by Hope Publishing Co., Carol Stream, IL 60188. All rights reserved. Used by permission.

with the demonstration or revelation theory of the atonement: namely, its tendency to deny the objective validity of what Jesus accomplished on the cross by making its effect wholly dependent upon our subjective human response. What Jesus does as our representative does not wholly depend upon whether or not we respond faithfully.

These are the kinds of considerations that make their way into the theological education that takes place in Church of the Crossroads as the members of the church seek to make a connection between their human experience of despair and suffering and the despair and suffering that Jesus experienced on the cross, as they seek to relate their lives to God. Such a seeking would not take place, however, were it not for the openness with which the members of the community share their lives and stories.

THE OPEN AND AFFIRMING COVENANT

The question arises: What is it, then, that accounts for this spirit of openness in Church of the Crossroads? In the end, it is all very mysterious, but one can point to some ingredients that make for this remarkable freedom to tell one's story within the community of faith.

At the same time (March 8, 1992) Church of the Crossroads adopted unanimously its Just Peace Covenant, it also adopted unanimously its *Open and Affirming Covenant*. This covenant reads as follows:

> We, the members of Church of the Crossroads, are a diverse community of people. We differ in age, gender, abilities, and sexual orientations. We hold varying theological and political beliefs and come from different socioeconomic and ethnic backgrounds. As a church community, we celebrate and find strength in that diversity and view it as a way to understand the inclusiveness of God.
>
> We recognize that, within both the church and the larger society, persons who differ in age, gender, social and ethnic background, sexual orientation, and physical and mental ability, have historically suffered persecution and continue to experience negative stereotypes, indifference to their needs, and rejection.
>
> We believe that, although we are many members, we are one body in Christ. As part of that body of Christ, we are called to love one another, to do justice, to bring release to the oppressed, and to walk humbly with our God. Responding to that call, one goal of our ministry is to heal the brokenness we experience in our relationships with each other and to witness our oneness in

Christ to the larger world through the inclusiveness of our own church community.

Therefore, we now publicly declare ourselves an "Open and Affirming Church," and set forth our beliefs and our intentions as a community of the faithful.

As regards social and ethnic background, we believe that we are "neither Greek nor Jew, male nor female" but brothers and sisters in the family of God. Our discipleship rests not on our age, gender, level of education, nor on economic and social success, but on our readiness to love God with all our heart, mind and soul, and to love our neighbors as ourselves. We further acknowledge that the cultural differences among us are rooted in generations of human history, offering a testimony to the rich variety of human experience, and revealing the many ways in which God has been made known to humankind.

As regards sexual orientation, we believe that we are made in God's image and that we are called to accept ourselves and our sexuality. Our sexuality is a gift of God, which, when expressed in mutual love, enriches our lives and deeply touches the reality of our own and others' humanity; it is one of the channels through which we experience life. All persons, regardless of sexual orientation, are entitled to express and receive human love and to receive the blessing of our church community in fostering committed relationships.

As regards persons of different abilities, we believe that each person is created in the image of God and is unconditionally loved as a child of God. The fullness of life experienced by an individual is determined by how one uses the talents and abilities entrusted to each by God. Each person is entitled to be treated with love and respect as part of the family of God.

We therefore commit ourselves, as a community of Christian people, to seek to end the continuing injustice and institutional discrimination, instances of violence, and denial of civil rights protection towards persons who differ in age, gender, social and ethnic background, sexual orientation, and physical and mental ability. We affirm that all such persons are welcome within the life of our church, to contribute their time, energy, and gifts to our common mission, including its employment and the leadership of the congregation. Furthermore, we seek to understand and respond to their special needs as they seek personal integrity, acceptance by their families, the church and the community, and the development of committed partnerships.

Of course, the words of such a covenant remain only words unless they are intentionally practiced. Yet, such a covenant can encourage a spirit of openness in a community of faith and can foster the kind of hospitality that is necessary if people are to be welcomed into the church and accepted for who they are. In fact, this covenant has made it possible for a number of people to feel secure enough to become members of the church community. Church of the Crossroads includes in its membership a number of gay and lesbian people, people who experience mental illness and physical disabilities, as well as persons who have someone who is gay or lesbian as a member of their families. These persons, for the most part, enter the life of the community ready to reveal their deeper selves and the joys and struggles of their lives.

OTHER FACTORS CONTRIBUTING TO A SPIRIT OF OPENNESS

Another factor that contributes to a spirit of openness in Church of the Crossroads is the size of its membership. Church of the Crossroads is a smaller community of faith with a membership of just over two hundred people. Over the years, I have detected an unspoken wish among the members of the church that it should remain the size it is. There is, for instance, a resistance to institute a second service of worship, although for a time an informal worship gathering took place on the first and third Sunday evenings of every month. This additional service for the most part included those who had already gathered together in the morning. The members of the community want everyone—children, youth, and adults, to gather at one time and in one place for worship. There is a feeling that a community of faith should be at least as good as the bar in the sitcom *Cheers*, a place "where everyone knows your name." At the same time, Church of the Crossroads is large enough for its members to sense "a critical mass" when everyone gathers in the church sanctuary. We at Church of the Crossroads are indeed fortunate. The church's sanctuary seats only about one hundred and fifty people comfortably. On a normal Sunday, around one hundred and twenty-five people gather for worship.

Another factor that encourages the spirit of openness is the pattern of leadership within the community. The pattern is more egalitarian than it is hierarchical. Leadership is exercised by the many rather than by the few. The unnamed leaders are as important as the named leaders. As decisions are made, the common good of all is uppermost on the minds of the decision makers. Differences are worked out in a consensus style of decision making. All of this encourages both a spirit of openness and also unity within the community.

There is also a conscious attempt to set aside patterns of control in favor of freedom. The members of the church are free to gather others together in groupings in order to pursue a specific activity or witness. The validity of the task or witness of each grouping is measured by participation rather than a careful scrutiny of the purpose of the group before it gets organized. Spontaneously, a group of women decided to meet in order to write out of their experience or perhaps in response to a particular sermon. The group, at my invitation, meets in the pastor's study following the Sunday service. Another group gathers for centering prayer in the sanctuary on Sunday mornings and at Monday noon in one of the meeting rooms; yet another centering prayer group has been meeting in a downtown location on Tuesday mornings. A psychologist trained in the art of narrative writing gathers together several members of the congregation along with members of the larger community monthly to write and share with one another the stories of their lives. There is no attempt to control these groups. The life of each group is encouraged and nurtured by one of the three mission teams organized to coordinate the mission and ministry of the church.

The care of the members of Church of the Crossroads is accomplished through the Crossroads Health Ministry and its parish nurse, Liz Nelson. This ministry was created three years ago to educate the congregation on issues related to health and wellness and also to respond to specific health needs of members and friends. Two additional groups support this ministry. Hui Manawaleʻa (meaning *group with a generous heart, that gives freely, that is benevolent*) provides one-to-one relationships between church members and those who need special care and attention. This group, now ten years old, relates to a larger interfaith care group, Project Dana, which was first established by the Buddhist community on the island of Oʻahu. A second group providing for the care of members is the Prayer Team. The names of church members and others who have special needs are included, with permission, in a confidential list sent each month to members who have made a commitment to pray daily for them.

Our Stories at the Foot of the Cross

PASTORAL LEADERSHIP

In these ways and others, a spirit of openness and hospitality is encouraged. I have come to believe that the pastor must model this same spirit, for how can there be openness in the church if the pastor himself or herself is not an open and welcoming human being? With this in mind, I now want to speak of my own leadership as pastor of the church. Everyone at Church of the Crossroads understands that my strength does not lie in administration. Fortunately, there are several members of the church who know how to do this well. My strength, perhaps, lies more in the kind of pastoral leadership I try to embody. I try, as best as I can, to do my work with a sense of humility, and not to think of myself more highly than I ought to think. I have come to believe that one of the real hazards related to pastoral ministry in our day is the elevation of the pastor in the context of the church. This is not to say that the office of pastor and teacher is not important in the church. To the contrary, the pastor occupies an important position in the church, not as one who seeks to control, however, but as one who encourages the leadership and ministry of others. The pastor must open himself or herself to the leadership and the theological insights of others in the community of faith. He or she must be as ready to be taught as to teach.

When it comes to encouraging the members of the church to speak of their despair and their hope in the telling of their stories, the pastor needs to set an example. The old style of pastoral leadership in which the pastor would never dare disclose his or her own struggles from the pulpit should be put to rest. Fortunately, I now enjoy the blessing of having been pastor of Church of the Crossroads for over nineteen years. The congregation has witnessed their pastor going through a number of transitions in his life, including a divorce, the death of a spouse, two marriages, the marriages of his daughters, and the births of five grandchildren. They have also come to know me as a person who struggles to be faithful, who seems to have as many doubts and questions as he has answers. All of these make their way into my conversations with members of the church and also into my preaching.

A SERMON

In the last chapter, I shared a sermon I preached following the momentous event of September 11, 2001. I now take the liberty of including yet another sermon, this one of a more personal nature. It was delivered on Sunday, September 10, 1995, less than two months prior to the death of my second wife, Becky Gallatin. The title of the sermon is *Making Whole* and the text upon which it is based is Psalm 139:1–24. It reads as follows:

> This week, I cannot help but approach the task of preaching in a slightly different way. There is a sense in which a preacher should always take into account the fabric of his or her own life when preaching, and also the nature of the world in which we live, and also the particular needs and issues present within the congregation. Today, however, the fabric of my own life overshadows the problems of the world and the issues we face in our congregation.
>
> Many of you are aware that the past few days have been most difficult for our family. Not only did we learn that Becky's cancer has recurred, but it seems to have recurred with a vengeance. This past Friday, she underwent surgery to remove water that had accumulated within the outer lining of her heart. It is almost certain that this problem arose because of the spreading of the cancer. The surgery did alleviate the difficulty she was experiencing with her breathing, and also her persistent cough. She is now resting comfortably and should be back home sometime this coming week. We hope there will be good days, weeks, months, and maybe years ahead.
>
> This recent medical crisis has forced us to make a shift in our thinking both about the present and the future. We have been led to make a journey further away from an optimistic attitude towards the future towards a hope that cannot deny the terrible reality of the disease Becky faces.
>
> Often in my preaching I have said that hope is given birth only in the midst of pain and suffering and that healing is not the same as curing. Becky's life and the life of our marriage and the life of our family now bear witness to that truth.
>
> Many of you have asked me what you can do to be helpful. In the days and weeks and we hope months to come, there may be little tasks that we will ask of you. We might ask you to run an errand or prepare a meal. For now, however, we ask only for your prayers and your presence. These gifts you have already given, and we are truly grateful. I know that you will continue to surround us with them.
>
> As your pastor, I need to say one more thing. You have given us the gift of your presence. I hope that you will not hesitate to call on me for my presence when it is needed. I am your pastor and I love being your pastor. My personal situation is difficult, yes, but

please do not deny my willingness to be with you when you need me. I have already had offers of help in the areas of preaching and administration. It is humbling, but I am convinced there are so many leaders at Crossroads that you could very well carry on the day-to-day worship and administrative responsibilities without me. But when you need me to sit down with you, or be with you in your home or in the hospital, let me know or have someone else let me know. It is important for me and for the church that I carry on with my pastoral responsibilities.

If you have read the novel *A Place on Earth*, you will recall how Wendell Berry portrays the daily, slow life of a farming community in which folk are deeply involved in each other's hurt. In the novel, Berry describes a human community in which people still have time for each other, in which the process of interaction between them is itself a healing. Berry is concerned that everyone in his story finds a place in the earth, in the land, in the fabric of human community and human experience. This is not a romantic novel, nor is it sentimental in its tone. In the story, there is a father who goes berserk as he watches his little daughter swept away by a flood. There is a handicapped, lonely carpenter who commits suicide over the wife of this same man. The novel does not cover over the destructive reality of human life, or the experience of hopelessness and despair which is part and parcel of human experience. The power of the novel is that it calls forth hope in the face of a harsh, brutalizing world.

The Feltners are the central family in the novel. It is the Second World War and Mat and Margaret Feltner have learned that their only son, Virgil, is "missing in action." He has been missing so long that the father grimly declares that Virgil is dead. When the town learns the news, the pastor, Brother Preston, must make his inevitable visit to the grieving family. The pastor wants to be a good pastor, but his visit does not work. The conversation is stiff and irrelevant. He is of little help. Everyone is relieved when his duty is done and his visit ends.

What went wrong? Back in the peaceful confines of the church building, the pastor knows that the visit has been a failure. *"He came away from the Feltner house grieved by the imperfection of his visit. It was not, as he had hoped it would be, a conversation. It was a sermon. This is the history of his life in Port William. The Word, in his speaking it, fails to be made flesh. It is a failure particularized for him in the palm of every work-stiffened hand held out to him at the church door every Sunday morning—the hard dark hand taking his pale unworn one in a gesture of politeness without understanding. He belongs to the governance of those he ministers to without belonging to their knowledge, the bringer of the Word preserved from flesh.*"[11]

During his visit with the Feltners, Brother Preston spoke not of earth but of heaven, "outside the claims of time and sorrow." Mat, the grieving father, without passing judgment on the pastor's effectiveness, observes that the pastor does not help because he offers the hope of heaven while, as he says, he "can only be comforted by the hope of earth." "*He is doomed to hope in the world, in the bonds of his own love. He is doomed to take every chance and desperate hope of hope between him and death, Virgil's, Margaret's, his. His hope of Heaven must be the hope of a man bound to the world that his life is not ultimately futile or ultimately meaningless, a hope more burdening than despair.*"[12]

Berry, the novelist, seems to be saying that healing, hope and the prospect of transformation, comes only in the course of daily life where pain is surfaced. Hope and healing do not come about by a grand scheme, but by human beings allowing themselves to be present in the hurt, by waiting in the hurt with honest speech and open grief, waiting and waiting, until the birth of hope that is strangely given, but never forced.

That is what Becky and I and the members of our families are learning. What little faith we have is not heaven-bent but earth-bound. For us, the turn from suffering to hope has not yet been given. We are simply "waiting in the hurt with honest speech and open grief, waiting and waiting."[13] One thing we do know. You are waiting with us. You are not giving us pious words, optimistic jargon or thoughts of heaven. You instead are giving us your waiting presence.

And I have a strange suspicion that your waiting presence with us is like God's waiting presence with us. Even though your presence is more real to us right now than the presence of God, every now and then I have a feeling that God also waits with us. And it may be one day we will experience the hope I so often mention in my preaching.

---

11. Berry, *A Place on Earth*, 97.

12. Ibid., 95.

13. As I was struggling to find the best words to convey my feelings in this sermon, I was drawn to Walter Brueggemann's book *Israel's Praise* (Fortress Press, 1988), and the part of the book in which he described *A Place on Earth*. I found that Brueggemann's words exactly described how I was feeling and so I have freely used them. I was particularly drawn to these words: "Human truth of a transformative kind happens not by a grand scheme, not by a floating archetype, but by the dailyness of being present in the hurt, by waiting in the hurt with honest speech and open grief, waiting and waiting, until the turn that is strangely given, but never forced," 131.

Our Stories at the Foot of the Cross

William Butler Yeats once wrote these lines:

> But Love has pitched his mansion in
> The place of excrement;
> For nothing can be sole or whole
> That has not been rent.[14]

Making whole will happen precisely where life is rent. That I believe. And beyond the making whole there is thanksgiving and the praise of God.

The other night a man wearing a "Jesus T-shirt" was walking through the hospital corridor saying in a loud voice, "Praise the Lord! Praise the Lord!" I thought to myself, "That's easy for you to say." I must admit I had the same reaction when I read and re-read Psalm 139 this past week, the appointed psalm for today that we read responsively this morning.

> For it was you who formed my inward parts;
> you knit me together in my mother's womb.
> I praise you, for I am fearfully and wonderfully made.
> Wonderful are your works; that I know very well.
> (Ps 139:13–14)

"That's easy for you to say." It is easy for you, the psalmist, to say that God knows you when you sit down and when you rise up, that God is with you always, that you find God everywhere you turn. Perhaps, however, the psalmist can say these things only because at one time his life had been rent. There is a hint of it in the psalm.

> If I say, "Surely the shadows shall cover me,
> and the light around me become night,"
> even the night is not without light to you;
> the night is as bright as the day,
> for the night is as light to you. (Ps 139:11–12)

Maybe the psalmist has known the darkness. Who can know? If the psalmist has known suffering and hurt and pain and has come through it to be made whole, then it is right to sound these words of praise. If the man who went through the hospital corridor speaking the words "Praise the Lord" has in his own life known the dark night of the soul, then perhaps it is right that he give praise.

But if praise is simply a cover-up, a way of avoiding the hurt and the grief, then praise is false and meaningless. I suspect that was the Brother Preston's problem in the novel. When he visited

---

14. Yeats, "Crazy Jane Talks with the Bishop," *The Collected Poems*, 259–60.

> the Feltners, he used praise as a cover-up. He could not allow himself simply to be present.
>
> As for us, we are waiting in the hurt with honest speech and open grief, waiting and waiting, until the birth of hope and healing. You are waiting with us. And every now and then, I have a feeling that God is waiting with us too. Thanks be to God.

Probably, by now, people have forgotten the content of this sermon other than the fact that I shared my own pain and struggle with the congregation. What is remembered, however, is what happened following the giving of this sermon. This sermon, and the ones that followed, served as an encouragement to other members of the community to share their own journeys, their experiences of loss, their own encounters with disease, not only breast cancer as was the case with my wife, but all kinds of illness. From those days on, something radically changed in the congregation for the better. The legacy of those days still informs the life of the community and also my own pastoral presence within the congregation.

GRACE AND THE NEW LIFE OF THE RESURRECTION

The sermon offered above is an example of how a theology of the cross can make its way into the preaching of the pastor and also into the life of the faith community itself. In the sermon, there is no talk about the Christ who "sits at the right hand of the Father" in glory. There is no talk of a God who is enthroned above the creation. There is only speech pointing tentatively to a God who waits with us in our own waiting. Yet, when I look back on that sermon preached nearly ten years ago and the human experience that accompanied it, something has changed. The suffering, disintegrated and raw at the time, has now in measure become integrated suffering.[15] How this process takes place cannot be easily explained. For the most part it remains a mystery. We do know that the process of integrating suffering into the fabric of our lives is a lifelong process. We do know that the process begins when the despair that does not know itself to be despair is named and spoken and acknowledged in the community of faith, or perhaps by some other community, even an extended family. Beyond this, though, we may say that it is only by the grace of God that human beings can come to terms with their suffering.

---

15. See Hall, *God and Human Suffering*.

Our Stories at the Foot of the Cross

Words that the Apostle Paul wrote to the Church in Corinth are instructive. He recalls an ongoing weakness described as a thorn in the flesh:

> ... to keep me from being too elated, a thorn was given me in the flesh, a messenger of Satan to torment me, to keep me from being too elated. Three times I appealed to the Lord about this, that it would leave me, but he said to me, "My grace is sufficient for you, for power is made perfect in weakness." So, I will boast all the more gladly of my weaknesses, so that the power of Christ may dwell in me. Therefore I am content with weaknesses, insults, hardships, persecutions, and calamities for the sake of Christ; for whenever I am weak, then I am strong. (2 Cor 12:7b–10)

Only one who can look back on his or her disintegrated suffering from the vantage point of integration would be able to say such a thing. But what if our Christian communities do not make room for despair and suffering? What if all of our human experience needs to be taken up into a theology of glory, into a suffering-free happiness? If this is the case, we will have missed the truth of the Gospel, that new life and hope is given only in the midst of suffering and despair. Christian communities committed to the transformation of human life will make room for the experience of despair and meaninglessness in the lives of their members. Walter Bruggemann's words bear repeating.

> Human truth of a transformative kind happens not by a grand scheme, not by a floating archetype, but by the dailyness of being present in the hurt, by waiting in the hurt with honest speech and open grief, waiting and waiting, until the turn that is strangely given, but never forced.[16]

Mysteriously, the "turn is strangely given," eventually. This is not only my experience, but it is also what I have observed in others. The loss, the hurt, the pain is never forgotten but, by the grace of God, it does become integrated into the ongoing journey that is life. This, surely, is resurrection.

One might begin to imagine Church of the Crossroads only as a place where despair is named and spoken. But it is not. It is a community in which transformation or resurrection is also experienced and celebrated. Church of the Crossroads could never be characterized as a somber community. It is a community that is awkward, uncertain, and doubtful at

16. Brueggemann, *Israel's Praise*, 131.

times, but it is also a community that is lively, celebratory, and even faithful, at other times. It is a community whose life and ministry and witness is informed and shaped by a theology of the cross, for it believes that it is in the cross itself that the new life of the resurrection is given. It is given there, simply because God is present there in the cross, offering transformation and new life, even as Jesus speaks his word of existential despair.

One might say that the stories of resurrection and transformation can only be told in retrospect, only after suffering has become integrated into our lives and experience. I believe the same holds true for faith communities. It has taken nearly three decades for Church of the Crossroads to integrate the disintegrative experience of the early seventies into its self-understanding as a community. We should not be surprised over this, however, for this was precisely the experience of the early Christian community following the death of Jesus. I have always been intrigued with the fact that the original version of Mark's gospel ends in confusion and bewilderment. Even as the resurrection is announced, there can be no integration of the news of the empty tomb into the lives of the disciples. It is only later that the disciples will be able to name their Easter morning experience as resurrection. That time did come for the disciples and it also comes for those who dare to wait upon God in the midst of their suffering. It is only later that they may come to understand that God was there, waiting with them, gifting them with resurrection.

5

Gathered for Worship

I like to look at the passages for the week with our lectionary study group and the pastor, reading them aloud in different translations with footnotes and other study helps, if available, letting the words rest and hearing what they draw out of our present lives in the world or our memories, and then together trying to discern a message or messages from the scripture passages before us—messages for ourselves as individuals, for the Crossroads community, and for the larger context. I always feel that this has been a worthy enterprise and "a good use of my time," to use a current buzz-phrase. Hearing fragments of our discussion in the Sunday sermon reinforces the feeling of having been part of a collective wisdom.

At other times, when I am disciplined in my spiritual practice, which, to be truthful, is not always, I read a brief scripture passage usually twice a day before Centering Prayer. Lately, I have been dipping into the Psalms, but sometimes I read selections from the lectionary readings for the coming week or read a few verses, working through one of the sections of the Hebrew Scriptures or the Newer Testament. Through these fairly minimal encounters with scripture for the past nine years as a practicing Christian and through others dimly remembered from childhood, I have gradually built up a fund of favorite passages that rise to the surface, bidden or unbidden, during times of challenge or as captions for our still beautiful creation.

—Margaret Brown

Following a life of faith without finding a foundation in scripture is like toiling in a garden where no seed has been planted. The lectionary study allows all to probe passages for bedrock. It is impossible for any individual to walk the entire field of any story or letter. Our gathering enriches all and allows each to reflect through the week and prepare the soil for Sunday. I enjoy fertilizing the fruits of the

Spirit, providing input to worship, and acting as a sounding board for Neal's musings.

—Larry Jones

What a joy to worship together in the spirit of Crossroads! I came to the church in the seventies to work as a substitute organist. As I experienced the gospel through word and music, this same spirit was working to transform a "job" into a "calling" to minister through music. It led me to experience new life in Christ, encounter seasoned wisdom, cultivate a stronger faith, and participate in a corporate awareness of God's healing power. The church has ministered unto me through its spirited worship and community, perhaps a good deal more than I have ministered unto it.

—Don Conover

Rejoice in the Lord always; again I will say, Rejoice. Let your gentleness be known to everyone. The Lord is near. Do not worry about anything, but in everything by prayer and supplication with thanksgiving let your requests be made known to God. And the peace of God, which surpasses all understanding, will guard your hearts and your minds in Christ Jesus. (Phil 4:4–7)

INTRODUCTORY REMARKS

THE WORSHIP LIFE OF communities of faith seeking to free themselves from the trappings of Christendom, which is an ongoing process and not easily accomplished, will pay great attention to how they worship God and why they gather together to do so. They will be consciously aware of both the manner and content of their worship. In their worship, they will be careful not to mimic the popular cultural forms of entertainment that are utilized by many churches out of the motivation to be successful and acceptable in the eyes of the larger culture. In our culture, the mode of entertainment exemplified by popular television programming has come to influence the way many Christian communities worship.[1] In much of this worship, performance and chatter have replaced mystery,

---

1. For an excellent analysis of television and its impact upon politics, education, religion, and the culture, see Postman, *Amusing Ourselves to Death: Discourse in the Age of Show Business.*

silence, the reading of scripture, and thoughtful preaching. Worshipers become passive recipients of everything that is being staged for them. The reading of scripture is reduced to one or two verses, and sermons often take the form of popular pep talks. Hymn books are discarded and the words of the songs sung are projected on large screens. Everything is geared for the video camera rather than for the complexity and depth of the act of worship.

At the same time, congregations seeking to move towards a more faithful future will not simply repeat the patterns of worship they have inherited from the past, just because "that's the way it's always been done." They will respect the patterns of worship that belong to their history and tradition, but they will also be ready and willing to shape a worship life that reflects the context in which they now find themselves. Their patterns of worship will arise out of their identity as communities of faith who embrace the process of disestablishment they are undergoing and who are discovering the possibilities that are being opened up to them as a result.

The communities of faith I have in mind will understand that the act of worship both sets them apart from the world in which they exist and also connects them to that same world, for it is the world as well as the Christian faith that shape the lives and experiences of their members. Worship, in a way, is a bridging act. It allows those who gather together to make a connection between God's story revealed through sacred scripture and the human story that both they and others in the world reflect. Thus, authentic worship must be contextual. It must take into account the context in which human beings find themselves, even as it seeks to connect God's story to human life.

Of course, worship begins and ends in doxology, in the praise of the God who created the earth and all that is in it (Psalm 24:1), who came to be with us in Jesus, Emmanuel, God-With-Us, who moves towards us and our existential despair in the cross, and who offers us, through the cross, hope and newness of life. Such praise glorifies God. Doxology is first and foremost a courageous and bold affirmation of the sovereignty of God that takes precedence over all other sovereignties and ideologies that seek to make a claim upon our lives and loyalties. As we sing the words of the Doxology, including the line that reads "praise God above ye heavenly host," we are declaring that all of our commitments to nation, community, family, and self must be evaluated in light of God's claim upon us.

Unfortunately, much of the praise offered in Sunday morning worship services in mainline churches is offered automatically without much thought or feeling, and therefore has little impact upon worshipers' lives. Perhaps it is the absence of feeling in so much of the praise offered in mainline churches that has given rise to the singing of so-called praise songs, but in these songs so much sentimental, individualized feeling is emoted that the praise of God again becomes a thoughtless act. Praise, rightly conceived, is an act that arises out of our encounter with the Spirit of God and the truth of the Gospel as we face the realities and needs of our own lives and the world.

Certainly, the praise of God is not the only thing that takes place in worship. Worship also has a teaching capacity. Through the act of confession, the hearing of scripture and the sermon, the offering of prayers of thanksgiving and intercession, and the coming together around the communion table, we human beings can come to understand better who we are and who we are meant to be. In the presence of God as we gather for worship, we can come to know both who we are and whose we are.

WORSHIP AT CHURCH OF THE CROSSROADS

I want to continue my reflections on the meaning that worship might have for a community of faith that is embracing this awkward moment in its life and ministry by describing an ordinary service of worship that one would experience if he or she were to gather with the congregation of Church of the Crossroads on most Sundays of the year. To do so, I have chosen a service that took place on June 13, 2004, the Second Sunday after Pentecost. Following the description of the service, I will comment upon the various aspects and parts of the service, and also will describe the planning that went into the shaping of the service.

I do all of this with humility. The worship life of Church of the Crossroads is not anything that could or should be imitated by other communities of faith. For one thing, patterns of worship constantly change and evolve, especially if due attention is paid to why and how we worship and the context in which we find ourselves. It would be a mistake, then, to describe a service of worship as if this is the way it should always be. For another thing, the worship life of any congregation will reflect that congregation's own identity and ethos because these are particular to any community of faith and arise out of its own history and its present location.

One would not anticipate the worship life of Church of the Crossroads to be the same as the worship life of other congregations. At the same time, there will be certain patterns and aspects of worship that will be common to communities of faith who are intentionally embracing the uncertainty of their present life, and who are seeking to identify themselves with a theology of the cross rather than a theology of glory.

On June 13, 2004, the scriptural texts that informed the worship were Isaiah 43:1–7, Psalm 5:1–8, Psalm 8, and Luke 7:36–50. In particular, the Gospel reading shaped the content of the service. In the reading, we encounter the story of the dinner given by Simon the Pharisee in honor of Jesus, and how the dinner was interrupted by a woman who entered the house, anointed the feet of Jesus with ointment, kissed them, and then dried them with her hair. The woman is shunned by Simon but received lovingly by Jesus. The main thought around which the worship was organized that day can be stated this way: *Although as human beings we know that we are honored by God who has created us, we are also subject to the experience of worthlessness and alienation; in the cross of Jesus, God moves toward us just as we are and offers us the gift of human authenticity.* Actually, this theme arose not only out of the scripture but also from a reading of Douglas John Hall's recent book, *The Cross in our Context,* in which he says, "*The cross reveals the compassionate determination of God to bring the human creature to the full realization of its potentiality for authenticity.*"[2]

THE SETTING

The theme of "that which constitutes our true humanity" was chosen in part because on this Sunday, June 13, two new banners were hung in the sanctuary for the first time. Both banners celebrate the beauty and diversity of the human beings who make up the community that constitutes Church of the Crossroads. Ellen Godbey Carson, who crafted the banners, had asked the members and friends of the church to contribute pieces of fabric that represented their ethnic backgrounds and heritages. With these, she created one banner that depicts a tree, the leaves of which are made from the various pieces of fabric. The other banner displays a circular pattern of human beings with their hands raised, each human figure made from a different piece of fabric. The figures are connected

---

2. Hall, *The Cross in our Context,* 105–6.

by a ribbon and a descending dove is included at the top of the banner. These banners are both celebratory and meaningful, and beautifully designed and crafted, I might add. These banners greeted the children and adults as they entered the sanctuary for worship on June 13, 2004. As people gathered, they anticipated that the worship service that day would explore the human dimensions of their life together in this particular community of faith.

Another element that informed the service on this Sunday was the fact that the Chancel Choir of the Chapel Hill United Church of Christ, Chapel Hill, North Carolina, was present. The members of this choir sang two anthems, and another anthem by the combined Chapel Hill choir and the Crossroads choir was sung. Because the Chapel Hill United Church of Christ is also an Open and Affirming Congregation of the United Church of Christ, I decided that the service should also celebrate the way that these two congregations intentionally welcome people who have not found acceptance in other Christian churches. In terms of planning, it is very difficult to achieve a unified worship experience when a visiting choir is present. The anthems did not exactly reflect the theme of the service. At the same time, the presence of the visiting choir was in itself a gift, simply because Church of the Crossroads often feels, wrongly I might add, that it represents a lone voice in the world of Christian churches. It is always good for the members of Church of the Crossroads to understand that there are other Christian communities that share their vision and commitments.

A COMPOSITION IN FOUR PARTS

I have come to understand that a service of worship can be likened to a drama consisting of four acts or a musical composition in four parts. These parts, stated simply, are *praise, confession, word,* and *response.* This has become the pattern of worship adopted by Church of the Crossroads over the years. Some find the pattern too predictable; others appreciate its predictability. In a world that is so often chaotic, most of the members of the congregation appreciate a service that grants a measure of order to their lives. I must add, however, that within each of the four parts of service, there is a freedom to depart from the usual. The tension between order and freedom is the kind of tension that makes room for creativity and the movement of the Spirit. Sometimes, a remarkable word is spoken, most often spontaneously as the sharing of a particular concern or experience, and this word is one that is not necessarily spoken by the pastor!

Part I: Praise

Gradually the members of the congregation arrive and take their places in the sanctuary. The older members of the congregation always arrive first; the younger members and families with children arrive at the last minute. Sometimes, one wonders whether or not there will be many coming in, but by the time worship begins, the sanctuary is quite full. As one might expect, there are whispers as members of the congregation greet one another. The pastor then walks to the front of the sanctuary and strikes a Buddhist gong three times. Immediately, the whispering ceases, and the entire congregation, including the children, becomes silent and attentive. The organist plays a voluntary that is appropriate for the church season as two children light the altar candles. The choir then sings an introit. On this Sunday, it is *Cantate*, by Giuseppe Ottavio Pitoni (1657–1743), a song of praise to God, the Maker of the "children of Sion." This is followed by the pastor saying, "The grace of our Lord Jesus Christ and the love of God and the communion of the Holy Spirit be with you all," to which the congregation responds, "And also with you."

One of the lectors leads a call to worship. On this particular Sunday, the call to worship is borrowed and adapted from Trinity United Church of Christ, an African American congregation located in Chicago, Illinois. The call celebrates the beauty of all the human beings who make up the creation and the honor that God has bestowed on them and all things.

> One: Beautiful are the works of God!
> Many: Beautiful also are the skins of God's people!
> One: Beautiful is the mind of God!
> Many: Beautiful also are the hopes of God's people!
> One: Beautiful is the heart of God!
> Many: Beautiful also are the souls of God's people!
> One: God made the heavens and the earth!
> Many: To God be the glory for the things God has done![3]

---

3. *The New Century Hymnal*, No. 824, used by permission.

A hymn of praise follows. "O How Glorious, Full of Wonder," a traditional hymn of praise for the beauty and wonder of creation, has been chosen particularly because it reflects the words of the 8th Psalm, a psalm that will be mentioned later in the sermon, and also because its third stanza speaks of both the grandeur and the misery that define the human being.

> You have set us in communion
> with the wonders of your hand,
> Made us fly with eagle pinion,
> pilgrims over sea and land.
> Soaring spire and ruined city,
> these our hopes and failures show.
> Teach us more of human pity,
> that we in your image grow.[4]

Following the hymn, the pastor speaks briefly with the children before they leave for their church school classes. Church of the Crossroads values the children who belong to its community and feels that it is important to have them as part of the worshiping congregation through the first part of the service.

Part II: Confession

Having sung its praise to God, the members of the community now enter into the act of confession. Sometimes, this act is introduced briefly by the pastor and a silence is then kept. On this Sunday, in keeping with the theme, the confession of sin is spoken by all and takes the form of a prayer originally composed by the poet and liturgist Arnold Kenseth and revised by the pastor. The prayer focuses on our failure to be the people God has created us to be.

> O God, we unburden ourselves before you, out of a need for a great mercy; for we have failed to be the people you created us to be. We have lied to ourselves about ourselves and worn masks and not trusted in love. We have been unfaithful to the goodness in others. We have dealt as misers with hope. We fret over illusions and refuse the realities that give us life. Yes, O God, we sin, we fail, we

---

4. Beach, 1958, rev. 1980; alt. by *New Century Hymnal*. No. 558, © 1958; renewed 1980, 1991 by the Estate of Curtis Beach, used by permission.

fall. Forgive us. Lift us up. Redeem us; through the grace of Jesus the Christ. Amen.[5]

This prayer truly reflects all that the members of Church of the Crossroads struggle to move beyond in their communal life. Following the prayer, a silence is kept.

The pastor then invites the congregation to stand in order to receive an assurance of their forgiveness. This assurance is just as important as the act of confession. The more inclusive pronoun "we" is used in the proclamation of forgiveness rather than the pronoun "I", as in "I announce to you. . . ." In other words, the pastor includes himself in the assurance of forgiveness. He too is forgiven! The pastor does not hurry through the words of the assurance as though they did not really matter. Following the assurance of forgiveness and in response to it, the pastor then invites the worshipers to extend the peace of Christ to one another. The members not only greet and embrace those who are standing nearby, but also others throughout the sanctuary, including the strangers in their midst. Then an act of praise is sung. On this Sunday, it is a rhythmic rendition of *Masithi*, the song of praise from the Christian community of South Africa which was first introduced to the worldwide church through the auspices of the World Council of Churches at its Seventh General Assembly in Canberra, Australia, in 1992. "*Masithi: Amen, siyakudumisa* ("Sing amen, we praise your name, O God.")[6] The worshipers do not need words or music; they have learned this song by heart.

Part III: Word

Having sung their praise to God, having confessed their sin, and having then received an assurance of God's forgiveness, the members of the congregation are ready to hear the words of the scriptures chosen for the day, most often, but not always, from the readings suggested by the Revised Common Lectionary.[7] On this Sunday, the pastor chooses a reading from

---

5. Kenseth, *Sabbaths, Sacraments, and Seasons*, 63. Alt. by D. Neal MacPherson, 2004.

6. Molefe, *The New Century Hymnal*, No. 760. Used by permission of Lumko Institute, South Africa.

7. *The Common Lectionary*, a three-year cycle of scripture readings for use in worship, was first developed in the mid-1960s by The Consultation on Common Texts (CCT), a forum for consultation on worship renewal among many Christian churches in Canada and the United States. In the lectionary, readings from the Hebrew and Christian scriptures are suggested for each Sunday and also for other holy days. *The Revised*

the Jewish scriptures different from the one suggested by the lectionary. It is Isaiah 43:1–7, chosen because it reflects the experience of exile and at the same time affirms the hope of restoration and the beauty and dignity of the human being:

> Do not fear, for I am with you;
> I will bring your offspring from the east,
> and from the west I will gather you;
> I will say to the north, "Give them up,"
> and to the south, "Do not withhold;
> bring my sons from far away
> and my daughters from the end of the earth—
> everyone who is called by my name,
> whom I created for my glory,
> whom I formed and made." (Isa 43:1–7)

Following the reading from Isaiah, the gathered community is invited to turn to the words of Psalm 5:1–8, the suggested psalm for the day, and read them silently. The congregation then listens as the Chapel Hill Choir sings the anthem *Lead Me, Lord* composed by Samuel Sebastian Wesley (1810–1876), the words of which are based upon the 8th verse of the psalm. "Lead me, Lord, in your righteousness because of my enemies, make your way straight before me." After a silence, the words of Luke 7:36–50 telling the story of Simon the Pharisee and the unnamed woman who anointed the feet of Jesus are then read. This reading is followed by the sermon.

The sermon I gave that Sunday began with a brief retelling of the story from Luke, in which I highlighted the contrast between Simon the Pharisee and the woman. I started by quoting a member of the congregation who often in conversation says that he isn't sure he would want to go to heaven because none of his friends will be there. I went on to say that if heaven is populated with people like Simon the Pharisee, I probably would not want to end up in heaven either! On the other hand, it would be a joy to be in heaven if it were populated by people like the woman, a forgiven sinner, who anointed the feet of Jesus. Why? Because she is presented in the story as a human being who is moving toward authenticity. "She sounds like an authentic human being to me—interesting,

---

Common Lectionary, providing a number of alternative readings, was published by the same ecumenical forum in 1992. *The Revised Common Lectionary* is now used widely by both Catholic and Protestant congregations.

extravagant in her loving, free with her emotions, free to be just who she is—a forgiven sinner overflowing with gratitude."

In the sermon, I described how it is Jesus, rather than Simon, who welcomes this woman into his presence, just as it was God who called and welcomed the ancient exiles home and honored them. Here, I also make reference to the words of Psalm 8, to the glory and honor God confers upon humankind in the act of creation. Human beings are created just a "little lower than God," and "crowned with glory and honor" (Ps 8:5).

In the sermon, I then turned to the context in which many human beings find themselves these days. They are excluded from church communities because they are "different." This is just one example of how human life itself has become devalued in our world.

> In our culture and in our world, human beings have become so dispensable and so denigrated that their lives count for nothing. We mourn the deaths of over seven hundred American soldiers in Iraq, but as yet have had no counting of the thousands upon thousands of Iraqi men, women, and children who have lost their lives as a result of this tragic, and I believe unnecessary, war. The lives of the Iraqi people literally seem to count for nothing. Nor do the homeless and hungry of our own communities. If they did count, we would consider their plight intolerable and unacceptable in this society of ours that prides itself on being humane.

Our own lives, also, are filled with "too much inhumanity, too much alienation, too much despair." These, however, are the realities with which we must live.

> Somehow, as human beings created in the image of God, we need to keep in dialectical tension our essential worth and dignity on the one hand, and our unavoidable brokenness on the other, both our grandeur and our misery as human beings.

Moving toward the central point of the sermon and referring to the writings of Douglas John Hall, I then continued:

> ... in the cross of Jesus we discover a God who identifies himself/herself both with our grandeur and our misery, our worthiness as human beings and also our brokenness. We discover a God who is with us and for us. Yet, there is more to say beyond this identification of God with the totality of our lives in the cross. Writes Hall, *"The cross reveals the compassionate determination of God to bring the human creature to the full realization of its potentiality for*

authenticity."[8] We can say that in the cross of Jesus Christ, God moves towards us and our brokenness, our despair, and grants us grace to embark on a journey towards authenticity, a journey toward becoming truly human. We will never quite arrive until we breathe in and out our last breath. Yet we are on this incredible journey towards becoming truly human, towards human authenticity.

The sermon concluded by referring back to the woman who anointed the feet of Jesus and the need for us to welcome the stranger into our midst.

> . . . One of the joys of being part of this Crossroads community, and I'm certain our guests from the United Church of Chapel Hill would say the same about their own faith community, is that we find ourselves in the company of brothers and sisters who know both the grandeur and misery of being human, who acknowledge both their essential dignity and also their brokenness, brothers and sisters who are just who they are, without pretense, brothers and sisters who shun religiosity in favor of human authenticity. Without such communities as our respective faith communities, I scarcely know how we would manage as human beings.
>
> So let us continue the journey together. Let us love much because we have been forgiven much. Let us be truly present for one another, just as God in Jesus the Christ has been with us and for us. So will we become the people, the truly authentic human beings God has created us to be. Amen.

Part IV: Response

Following the sermon, a hymn of response is sung. On this Sunday, it is a song that arose out of the Mexican-American experience and especially the struggle of the United Farm Workers to form a union in parts of the United States. The song, sung in both Spanish and English, is called *De Colores* (Sing of Colors), and the English rendition of the second stanza celebrates a compassionate God, a loving Christ, and the variety and beauty of both human and extra-human life.

> Sing rejoicing!
> Every creature that breathes raise a song to the God of creation.
> Sing, rejoicing!
> Sing to God who so earnestly cares, who has offered salvation

---

8. Hall, *The Cross in Our Context*, 105–6.

Gathered for Worship

> Sing the good news!
> Sing the love of the Savior reflecting the colors of all.
> Many colors that shine from God's face,
> Many colors that tell us God's love to recall. . . .[9]

The hymn is followed by words of welcome, a few announcements, and then the pastor invites the community to enter a time of prayer. He announces some concerns that have arisen both from the context of the world and from the lives of members of the congregation. By doing so, the pastor suggests that our prayers of intercession are not given in the expectation that all will be cured, but rather are offered in the hope that one day all will be well, and also that the response to these prayers will be evidenced in our care for one another and our faithful witness in the world. Others are then invited to mention their own concerns for themselves and for the world. Following this, a brief prayer of thanksgiving is given, and then a time of silence in which the concerns that have been spoken can enter into the act of prayer, along with prayers that have not been spoken but which are "written upon the heart." The silence is concluded with the Lord's Prayer, which is said in unison.

The offering is then received; on this Sunday, the combined choirs sing an anthem. Following the singing of the Doxology in the Hawaiian language, a prayer is given by one of the lectors, and a concluding hymn is sung. At this service, the hymn chosen to conclude the service is Brian Wren's beautiful hymn *May the Sending One Defend You*. The words of this hymn reflect a summing up of all that has been said and sung throughout the service of worship.

> May the Sending One defend you,
> may the Seeking One amend you,
> May the Keeping One befriend you,
> in your gladness and in your grieving.
>
> May the Given One retrieve you,
> may the Gifted One relieve you,
> May the Giving One receive you,
> in your falling and your restoring.
>
> May the Binding One unite you—
> may the One Beloved invite you—

---

9. Mexican folk song, arr. Alfredo Morales, transl. *The New Century Hymnal*, No. 402. © 1995 The Pilgrim Press. All rights reserved. Used by permission.

May the Loving One delight you—
three in One, joy in life unending.[10]

I, as pastor, then give the benediction. On this particular Sunday, as on most Sundays, it is preceded with words of a dismissal based on Romans 12:9–21 and 1 Thessalonians 5:12–21. These words have become important for all who gather for worship at Church of the Crossroads.

> Let us now go forth in peace.
> Let us hold fast to that which is good,
> never paying back wrong for wrong,
> but encouraging the faint-hearted,
> supporting the weak and the distressed.
> giving due honor to every person
> and to all the things of the earth.
> And let us rejoice in the Spirit,
> pray continually,
> giving thanks in all circumstances,
> for this is what God in Christ wills for us.
> And may God's blessing be upon us
> and upon our world, forever. Amen.

The altar candles are extinguished by two children as the organist plays a closing voluntary. I feel that it is important for children to both light and extinguish the altar candles because this little act is both a way to include them in the worship of the gathered community and also a way to remind children (and adults, for that matter) that the light of God is not confined to the church. The light is brought into the church from the world at the beginning of the service and is taken back out into the world at its close. We must also be where the light is, whether in the world or in the church.

THE CENTRALITY OF SCRIPTURE

At Church of the Crossroads, in the act of worship, considerable importance is given to the word that is read and preached. There has been a denigration of the written and spoken word in our contemporary society. Words have become cheapened as a result of the ideological talk that dominates political discourse and the way that the consumer society uses

---

10. Wren, 1989, rev. 1993. Words © 1989 by Hope Publishing Co., Carol Stream, IL 60188. All rights reserved. Used by permission.

words to sell this or that. At the same time, words are powerful. When God speaks, the world comes into being; and when God speaks a word of judgment, the worth and dignity of human beings are called into question. In like manner, the word of the prophet can both create and destroy.

> Then the Lord put out his hand and touched my mouth;
> and the Lord said to me,
> "Now I have put my words in your mouth.
> See, today I appoint you over nations and over kingdoms,
> to pluck up and to pull down,
> to destroy and to overthrow,
> to build and to plant." (Jer 1:9–10)

This passage from the prophets is a reminder that we do not possess the "Word" spoken by God in the scriptures; the "Word" possesses us. In like manner, the Gospel ("Good News") is not something we can contain, control, or own. It is something that has the power to *shape and change us* if only we allow its truths to inform our lives.

The church often contributes unwittingly to the denigration of the spoken word, which is so powerful in the Judeo-Christian tradition, when it organizes so-called contemporary worship services largely for those who belong to "Generation X." Contemporary worship is somewhat of a misnomer, for surely all worship is contemporary simply because it takes place in the present. Beyond the questionable nomenclature, what one finds in these services is less scripture and preaching and more and more praise songs. I fear that in organizing these kinds of worship services, the church is creating a whole new generation of illiterate Christians.

My sermons are always written in advance in manuscript form. Printed copies are available on the same Sunday that the sermon is preached, before the service. This not only aids those who are hearing impaired, but the more noteworthy sermons then become a source of ongoing reflection for the members as they begin a new week. Often, for example, a women's writing group that meets in the pastor's study following the service will reflect upon the theme of the sermon and then commit their thoughts and reflections to writing. On occasion, a sermon is important enough to receive an even wider hearing as members send it to friends or as it is posted on the church's web site.

The development of the service of worship and the sermon is a weeklong process. On Monday morning, I carefully read the lectionary readings for the coming Sunday. These readings then become the focus of the lectionary study group that meets Monday afternoons. At the beginning of this chapter, you will find two reflections on the importance of the lectionary study group for the worship life of the congregation. The context of the world and human life lived in the world are taken seriously by the group. God's story embedded in the scriptures is brought into dialectical tension with our human experience. Gradually, one or two themes emerge from what is shared in the study group, and I carry these themes with me into the rest of the week. In the next day or so, as I further reflect on the needs of the congregation and the world, and also upon the context of my own life, one of the themes comes to the surface and is chosen. I may choose to have all the lectionary readings included in the actual service or just some of them. There are times when the thematic unity of the service is best served by choosing an alternative reading that is not suggested by the lectionary.

I have found over the years that the lectionary is sometimes a blessing and sometimes less so. The lectionary forces me and the members of the community to consider scriptural passages we might otherwise want to avoid. At the same time, it is sometimes difficult to relate the suggested scriptures to our lived human experience in our particular time and place. I have come to believe that the lectionary is best taken seriously, with the provision that it should be set aside when particular events and experiences or the development of a theme calls for a departure from it.

By the time Tuesday afternoon arrives, I am ready to meet with the Minister of Music. Together, we review the theme of the service and then choose the hymns. The unity of the service is achieved most often through the selection of the hymns along with the call to worship and the prayer of confession. An appropriate anthem is then chosen for the service. Our minister of music, Don Conover, has reviewed the lectionary readings in advance, and he will have four or five anthems on the "back burner." At the weekly choir rehearsal on Wednesday evening, one of these anthems will be prepared for the coming Sunday.

On Thursday and Friday of each week, the other parts of the service, including the prayers, are shaped and the scripture readings are given to the lectors. Resources from the United Church of Christ, the Iona Community, the Taizé Community, and the World Council of Churches are used. Prayers from the New Zealand Prayer Book, the Book of Common Prayer, including the Book of Alternative Services, as well as the Book of Worship of the United Church of Christ also find their way into the service. Finally, an order of service is written out. Usually, the sermon is prepared in final form on Saturday, although it has been in the works all week long. As I reflect on the planning that goes into the Sunday service, I am reminded of the word *leitourgia*, the Greek word that means literally "the work of the people." The development of the liturgical life of a community of faith is truly hard work. A great deal of thought and intentionality needs to go into it, not just on the part of the pastor, but on the part of many others as well.

SOUND AND SILENCE

Each service of worship at Church of the Crossroads begins in silence once the Buddhist gong is struck. The story behind the introduction of the gong into the worship life of Crossroads is interesting. The idea occurred to me after attending a Buddhist memorial service for the mother of a good friend at the main temple of the Honpa Hongwanji Buddhist Mission in Hawai'i. A large community was gathered for the service and, as one would expect, a quiet hum of chatter was heard throughout the temple as the friends and members of the bereaved family greeted one another. Then, the large temple gong located on the porch of the temple was struck and all chatter ceased at once. A silence came over everyone, and the attention of all was directed to the movement of the priests before the image of the Buddha and the beginning words and chants of the service. I thought to myself, "We can learn something from the Buddhists! If the Buddhist community can be brought to silence by means of a gong, surely this would be possible also at Crossroads." I introduced the idea to the church, and subsequently Phyllis Roe, a member of the congregation at the time, obtained a suitable gong while on a trip to Japan with the assistance of the Rev. Yoshiaki Fujitani, a former bishop of the Honpa Hongwanji and a good friend of the Crossroads community. The sounding of the gong has begun worship at Church of the Crossroads ever since.

I am convinced that silence must be built into the worship of communities of faith as they make their way through this time of transition in their life, ministry, and mission. The worship of Protestant churches has been so filled with talk and chatter that there has been little room for the act of listening and the need to be attentive to the leading of the Spirit. In the church of my grandparents and my own parents, it was simply assumed that everyone would be silent prior to worship. The presence of others might be acknowledged but only nonverbally or with a whisper that could not be heard by anyone else. I have often wondered why we seem to have a need to be so chatty in our present-day churches. It may be a result of the instant communication age in which we live. No one waits to have a conversation. Now, all we need to do is to call someone on our cell phones. It is not easy to re-introduce silence into our worship gatherings, but I find that when we do, it is welcomed as though silence were really something we truly need in our lives. At Church of the Crossroads, some of the people who are most involved and active in issues of peace and justice in the world are the ones who are most drawn to silence and meditation. As the years go by, the silences introduced into the service have been appreciated more and more. In the beginning, one would hear the sounds of nervous shuffling of paper and feet each time a silence was included in the service. Now, except for the ever-present traffic noise, one notices the deepening quality of the silence. There is something in us that longs for and covets the gift of silence, and something both ordinary and extraordinary takes place when it is experienced in the company of others.

In this regard, we have much to learn from the Quaker community as well as the Buddhist community. Both listening and attentiveness are needed if we are going to hear anew what the Spirit is saying to the churches in the new context in which they find themselves. "Prayer," Simone Weil writes, "consists of attention."

> It is the orientation of all the attention of which the soul is capable toward God. The quality of the attention counts for much in the quality of the prayer. Warmth of heart cannot make up for it.[11]

She goes on to say that attentiveness is not only necessary to the life of prayer, but also to the way we perceive the order of the world and the way we love our neighbor. "The soul empties itself of all its own contents in order to receive into itself the being it is looking at, just as he is, in all his truth."[12]

One cannot be attentive unless one is passive. The sounding of the gong at the beginning of worship is a reminder that, in worship, we find ourselves waiting for God, in a sense. We become passive so that we may receive something that is new and instructive for our lives and the life

---

11. Weil, *Waiting for God*, 58.
12. Ibid., 65.

of our community. This *passivity* associated with attentiveness may be contrasted to the constant *activity* which has not only dominated our lives but also the life of our churches. Speaking of the link between human activity and muscular effort and the need for passivity in our lives, Simone Weil writes,

> In our acts of obedience to God we are passive; whatever difficulties we have to surmount, however great our activity may appear to be, there is nothing analogous to muscular effort; there is only waiting, attention, silence, immobility, constant through suffering and joy. The crucifixion of Christ is the model of all acts of obedience.[13]

Simone Weil likens this kind of passivity to that which is described in the Bhagavad-Gita and also by Lao Tse. Buddhism also teaches this same need for passivity in our lives. In fact, the sounding of a Buddhist gong itself serves to bring worshipers to attentiveness, and not only that, but attentiveness to the transitory and limited nature of all existence. Just as the sound of the gong gradually fades and becomes no more, so it is with our lives.

> You turn us back to dust,
> and say, "Turn back, you mortals."
> For a thousand years in your sight
> are like yesterday when it is past,
> or a watch in the night.
>
> You sweep them away; they are like a dream,
> like grass that is renewed in the morning;
> in the morning it flourishes and is renewed;
> in the evening it fades and withers. (Ps 92:3–6)

The sounding of the gong, then, at the beginning of the service is not only a call to silence and attentiveness, but also a call to passivity and a relinquishing of control, both of which are required if we are to be obedient to the leading of God's Spirit in this time of endings and beginnings in the life of our churches.

At Church of the Crossroads, we are gradually coming to understand that silence needs to be introduced throughout the service of worship. Brief silences are kept at the end of each reading of scripture so that the words can find their way into the hearts and minds of those who are listening. We

13. Ibid., 126.

have also sought to introduce extended periods of silence into worship. Silence is kept during the time when prayers of intercession are offered for others. In 2004, during the season of Lent, a four- to five-minute silence was observed following the reading of the Psalm. A twenty-minute silence is also kept each of the three times during the week that people gather for centering prayer. Gradually, we are becoming a people who are willing to listen as well as a people who are led to speak.

DOXOLOGY

If attentiveness and silence belong to the life of prayer, then it is true that song belongs to doxology, to the praise of God. Worship includes both prayer and praise. And just as prayer without silence becomes an empty mouthing of words, praise that is separated from the context of life lived in the world becomes empty praise.

Not too long ago, I visited a church only to discover that all the furnishings in the chancel, including altar, pulpit and lectern, had been removed and replaced by sound equipment and acoustic guitars. The first half hour of the service in this church was devoted to praise music. The eyes of the attractive young singers were focused upwards. The eyes of the "audience" were focused on the simple, repetitive, somewhat mindless lyrics that were projected on a large screen. I felt somewhat uncomfortable, not knowing why, until I realized that for me, if not for others, all of this praise served as a kind of escape from the real context of life as it is lived and experienced. For me, this kind of praise negates the meaning I have discovered in the theology of the cross. I also realized that for me, these acts of praise somehow negated the incarnation. It was as if the music was being sung in order to bring God into the worship, as if God had not already come to us in Jesus the Christ. Praise of this sort served to manufacture the presence of God in that particular setting of the church.

Contrasted to this kind of inauthentic praise is the genuine praise that arises out of the hope that is granted to us in the midst of despair. Such hope, which gives rise to the act of praise, does not come easily to an exiled people who are experiencing their disestablishment in the world. We need only to recall the opening words of the 137th Psalm.

> By the rivers of Babylon—
> there we sat down and there we wept
> when we remembered Zion.

> On the willows there we hung up our harps.
> For there our captors asked us for songs,
> and our tormentors asked for mirth, saying,
> "Sing us one of the songs of Zion!"
>
> How could we sing the Lord's song
> in a foreign land? (Ps 137:1–4)

If our praise of God arises out of a deeply felt and believed hope that has been born in the midst of the despair we experience in our lives and in the world, then our praise of God is genuine and has integrity. As Walter Brueggemann has taught us, such praise can even serve as a protest against the false claims and optimism of the empire in which we find ourselves. The praise of God is not the praise of Caesar. This kind of genuine praise becomes a central act and declaration of communities of faith who are embracing the process of their disestablishment, who have come to know themselves as being *in* the world but not *of* the world.

More and more, our praise at Church of the Crossroads arises out of this understanding, out of a hope that is given birth in the midst of despair, when such a hope becomes possible. At times, the members of the community for whom this hope is not yet a possibility must rely upon the praise of others for whom such a hope has become possible, who have come to a time when they can sing the words of the traditional Shaker hymn:

> My life flows on in endless song
> Above earth's lamentations,
> I hear the real, though far-off hymn
> That hails a new creation.
> Through all the tumult and the strife
> I hear its music ringing.
> It sounds an echo in my soul
> How can I keep from singing?[14]

Such praise belongs to a theology of the cross and cannot be sung, or will not be sung, by a triumphant church. This has become the music and praise of Church of the Crossroads.

The hymns of praise that are sung at Church of the Crossroads are chosen carefully and deliberately in consultation with others. As has been described, they are chosen while attention is paid to the main theme of

---

14. Anon. "How Can I Keep from Singing?" *The New Century Hymnal*, No. 476.

each service and the human and world context out of which that theme has emerged. This is not to say that everything works well each time the community gathers for worship. Sometimes, less than adequate choices are made, but these only come to light in retrospect, most likely on a Sunday afternoon or Monday morning!

COMMON PATTERNS

It now may be possible to draw together some characteristics that will be common to the worship life of Christian communities who consider the present time of uncertainty in their life and mission as opportunity rather than burden. In the first place, the worship life of these communities will be *ecumenical* in spirit. The worship service, I am convinced, must be able to reflect the human experience and hopes of those who gather, as well as the Story that shapes the life of Christian communities. Christian communities willing to embrace their disestablishment in the world will find themselves comprised of thinking people from a variety of mainline Protestant traditions, as well as the Roman Catholic tradition. At Church of the Crossroads, we say that practically everyone is a "former something." We can count the number of people who were born and raised Congregationalist on one hand! Episcopalians, Catholics, Methodists, Lutherans, Baptists, as well as those who have had no church experience, make up the membership of the congregation.

It is important for the service of worship to reflect a wider ecumenical world than just Congregationalist patterns of worship that existed before the *United Church of Christ Book of Worship* was introduced into the life of the churches. For this reason, the Revised Common Lectionary, an ecumenical resource, is used, as well as prayers and liturgies from other Protestant traditions. Because the pattern of praise, confession, word, and response is found in the liturgical forms in many Protestant liturgical traditions as well as in the Roman Catholic mass, those who come to Church of the Crossroads from all those traditions have the experience of "coming home," even if they have been absent from church for a long time. The ecumenical spirit of worship at Church of the Crossroads is also reflected in the fact that other kinds of services are introduced now and then, including the services and music of the Holden Village and the Taizé Communities. Also, an Easter Vigil, often associated with more liturgical churches, is celebrated each year at Church of the Crossroads.

Gathered for Worship

The ecumenical spirit of the worship at Church of the Crossroads has more value than just making it comfortable for people from a variety of liturgical traditions to enter into the Sunday service. Its value also lies in the fact that it connects us to the larger Christian community beyond the confines of our own church. It opens us to a larger world of faith and worship. We sense that we are part of a movement that includes many others from whom we can learn and with whom we can join as we seek to be God's faithful people in the world.

Secondly, the planning of worship in the communities of faith I have in mind will be filled with much *intentionality*. In the planning of worship, every aspect of worship is carefully considered. After all, in a time when the church faces the uncertainty and awkwardness of its changing status in the world, the church must pay considerable attention to how it engages in the worship of God and how it participates in God's mission in the world. Everything should be questioned and examined so that our worship and our witness truly reflect who we are and who we are called to be as communities of faith. The preparation for any worship gathering must be done intentionally and with great care.

Thirdly, the worship life of communities who are ready to embrace this awkward moment in their lives will speak to both *heart* and *mind*. The music of worship, the visual aspects of the worship setting, the prayers that are offered, and the words that are spoken will involve the human being in his or her wholeness. The community in worship will be free to weep in times of loss and rejoice in times of joy. The bodies of the worshipers will be poised in anticipation. The minds of those who gather for worship will be both challenged and engaged. The concerns of those who come to worship will be heard and honored.

Fourthly, the worship life of the communities of faith I have in mind will be *contextual* worship. Because a theology of the cross rather than a theology of glory will be at the center of these communities, their worship will lead them towards the One who, on the cross, represents our and the world's despair and brokenness, and also our and the world's hope for restoration and transformation. A theology of glory tends to separate worshiping communities from their worldly and human context simply because it encourages an otherworldliness that hinders a faithful engagement with the world. Because the theology of the cross focuses on life as it is actually experienced in the world, our human situation in the world will necessarily enter into the sanctuary with us on a Sunday morning.

Therefore, our worship will always pay attention to the context in which we live. Furthermore, the world itself will be listening in to our services of worship. I am always aware that the strangers who position themselves at the edge of the worshiping congregation represent a curious and listening world. At Church of the Crossroads, these folk often remain on the porch of the church, listening in to the service. Through them, our worship addresses not only those who gather as part of the community of faith, but also the world itself.

This leads me to suggest a fifth common element in the worship life of communities of faith who intentionally embrace their changing status in the world. Their services of worship will be *evangelical* in spirit. I use the word "evangelical" somewhat cautiously because I am aware that it has come to mean something different from what it meant originally. "Evangelical" has come to be associated with conservative, "born again," even biblically fundamentalist Christian believers and communities.

Originally, the word was simply used to describe Christian believers and communities who were committed to the "good news" of the Gospel. The spirit of the worship service I described in this chapter would not be considered evangelical by the churches that are now known by this name. Yet, the worship life of Church of the Crossroads is evangelical in the best sense of the word, for it does represent the good news of the Gospel, that in the cross of Jesus, God moves towards us in our humanity, in both our grandeur and in our misery, and offers us a way towards human authenticity. What could be more evangelical than that?

The worship life of the changing communities of faith will also be evangelical in the sense that it will lead these churches to engage the world with that same good news of the Gospel. For these communities to do so, however, they must see themselves as being *in* the world but not *of* it. A church caught up in the false hope of progress and success so prevalent in the officially optimistic society surrounding it will have very little to say to the world. Only a church centered in a theology of the cross, which finds itself in dialectical tension with the false hopes of the culture, will have something to say that reflects the good news, the *evangel* of the Gospel.

6

The Spirit of Crossroads

To me, receiving Communion at Church of the Crossroads feels like participating in a joyous feast where truly people come from all the corners of the earth. Young and older, children and adults, those who are physically challenged, people with names like Aoki, Dye-Chiew, Guanson, Chang, de St. Croix, Laeha, Lee, Napua, Mukaida, Tiogangco, Viglielmo, Rantala, Nagamori, Wilson, Wong, and Young walk up to the table. I love watching their faces and recognizing everyone.

—Kikue Takagi

Listen to someone say the word "baptism" and usually one of two images comes to mind: a sparkling river, folks dressed in white singing on the banks, a fervor-filled sinner being plunged down beneath cool waters to emerge cleansed and joyous, shouting and praising God with a loud voice and hands upraised; or a solemn gathering of family and friends around proud parents who hold their infant at the font so that it can be gently sprinkled with holy water in the name of each person of the Trinity.

When it came time for my baptism, neither of these options was open to me. I was an adult in my mid-thirties and the tradition for baptism at my church was not full immersion. Still, like an infant to whom everything is new, I was nervous and a little appalled at the thought of being baptized before the whole community at Church of the Crossroads during the Easter Vigil of 1993. Although I loved God and this community who had taught me and shown God to me, I was still a little shy at the thought of such a public declaration of my desire to be a committed Christian (in a world that does not seem to support commitment to anything, but especially to a faith-based ethics). I was also nervous at so publicly declaring my love for the Crossroads community because I knew that I was opening my heart and my life further to the claims that their witness would make on me, and I was unsure that I had talents or the courage to bring to such a relationship.

I suppose it was a leap of faith on both our parts.

When the evening came, I dressed carefully. I even did something about my hair which tends to be unruly. I tamed it with multiple layers of hair spray. At the appropriate time, I stood beside the font (which is just outside the chancel). When asked, I promised to resist evil and to love God. I promised that I would try to make my life a reflection of the love and blessings that God pours out to me every day. I promised to be a disciple of Christ.

Having made all of those promises, I was ready to be washed and made ready for my new life as part of the Body of Christ. Neal, my pastor, proceeded to scoop out handfuls of water which he dumped onto my head, first in the name of the Father (but I felt nothing), and then the Son (still nothing), and finally, in the name of the Holy Spirit. It was sometime during the pronouncement of the last part of the Trinity that the water finally penetrated the layers of hair spray that had created a hair helmet on my head, and finally, the water began to drip down onto my scalp. It was an odd sensation and rather cold, but once it had gotten through, it began to drip into my eyes, down my neck, back and temples, and onto my shoulders.

Before my baptismal evening, Neal told me that it was only going to be a few handfuls, but that he was going to pour enough water onto me so that I would know I was wet. He was right. I did then, and it seems to me that the waters of baptism continue to soak in long after they are poured out. The water of baptism finds and cuts new channels into the life that is fed and nurtured with encouragement and example. I am grateful and I hope this is what will continue to happen for me.

—Jeannie Thompson

I have been a member here for thirty-five years, which is a pretty long time. One moment in the church that took place about thirty years ago seems to me to say what I find so wonderful about this church, and that is its openness. It was an Easter Sunday, and we had at that time responses to the sermons, and I believe it was Mr. Watada who stood up and said that he didn't understand why we had to have Easter, that for him the life of Jesus was so wonderful that even if it ended with Good Friday, that was enough. I was struck with the fact that he had the courage to say what he did. I couldn't really imagine any other church at that time where a person could say that and still be considered a member of the church. John Cobb, the preacher on *that Easter Sunday, answered very pleasantly without the slightest hint of being shocked by the question. He said that he understood where the question was coming from, but that for him, Easter was an important part of the message and he went on to say why this was so for him.*

—Val Viglielmo

You are the salt of the earth; but if salt has lost its taste, how can its saltiness be restored? It is no longer good for anything, but is thrown out and trampled under foot.

You are the light of the world. A city built on a hill cannot be hid. No one after lighting a lamp puts it under the bushel basket, but on the lampstand, and it gives light to all in the house. In the same way, let your light shine before others, so that they may see your good works and give glory to your Father in heaven. (Matt 5:13–16)

And again he said, "To what should I compare the kingdom of God? It is like yeast that a woman took and mixed in with three measures of flour until all of it was leavened." (Lk 13:20–21)

THE SPIRIT OF A COMMUNITY

Thus far in this book, I have described a particular church's history and have spoken about its engagement with the world. I have described the way in which its members are encouraged to get in touch with their own stories, the reality of their lives and their hopes. I have depicted the ways in which the congregation gathers for worship. As I have written about Church of the Crossroads, I have also tried to speak of the larger social and cultural context in which a church like Church of the Crossroads exists. I have written in the hope that this little book will spark the imaginations of its readers so that they will be encouraged to reflect upon the history and present life of their own faith communities. I also hope that the readers of this book will take seriously the need for the church to embrace a theology of the cross rather than a theology of glory as it seeks to carry out its life and mission, and that they will see the process of Christendom's disestablishment not as a burden but as an opportunity.

In this closing chapter, I would like to describe the life, the ministry and mission of Church of the Crossroads in yet another way, again in the hope that the reader will be led to reflect on the life and spirit of his or her own community of faith. I want to speak of the *ethos* of Church of the Crossroads. The *American Heritage Dictionary of the English Language* defines *ethos* as "the disposition, character, or fundamental values peculiar to a specific person, people, culture, or movement."[1] The ethos of any community of faith is informed both by how others see the community and by how it is seen by those who belong to it. I will begin with the perceptions those in the larger community have of Church of the Crossroads and then discuss the ways in which its own members speak of its ethos. Ultimately, it is the members of a community of faith who shape its spirit and character.

In the larger community, those who know about Church of the Crossroads often speak about its reputation as a church that is involved in the pressing issues of the day. Crossroads has been described by some as a weathervane: "If you want to know which way the winds of change are blowing, just look at Church of the Crossroads." If they come from secular people, these kinds of comments testify to our church's history of engagement with the world. These folk see Church of the Crossroads as an ally in the struggle for justice and peace in our world. I am glad we are seen in that way.

At the same time, some of the impressions others have of Church of the Crossroads are simply unfounded and without merit. For example, some people who are members of other Christian churches have said to me, "I have heard that you people do not pay much attention to the Bible," or "Some say that you do not take Jesus seriously at Crossroads." These kinds of comments reveal more about the persons making the comments than they accurately describe Church of the Crossroads. They reflect conventional Christianity's view that if a congregation is involved in a social witness in the world, especially around issues of justice and peace, it surely cannot be taking the Bible or Jesus all that seriously. They also make their comments out of a belief that Christianity's primary focus should be upon the salvation of individual persons.

It is indeed puzzling that in conventional Christianity, the Bible has come to stand for a form of piety that shuns involvement in the world

---

1. *American Heritage Dictionary of the English Language*, 4th Edition.

The Spirit of Crossroads

and a concern for the stewardship of creation. A reading of the Hebrew prophets and the words spoken by Jesus cannot help but evoke a commitment to peace and justice in our world. Jesus himself spoke more about wealth and poverty than any other subject! For the annual Martin Luther King, Jr. service and celebration at Church of the Crossroads, we have no trouble finding suitable passages of scripture to be read.

How, then, has it come to be that others would assume that Church of the Crossroads, because of its witness for peace and justice in the world, cannot, therefore, have much regard for the Bible? I suggest two possible reasons. First, the so-called liberal churches of Protestantism, the very churches most likely to be involved in social witness, have not taken the Bible as seriously as have more conservative churches. This neglect of the Bible in mainline Protestantism can be attributed, in part, to a popular and unfounded notion that modern, thinking Christians could not possibly put much stock in such a book. The Bible has been so analyzed and deconstructed by teachers and scholars in the seminaries belonging to mainline Protestantism that the members of our churches have come to see it as a book filled with mythical stories, inconsistencies, contradictions, and half-truths. Such a book cannot be taken seriously, they have thought.

Actually, the tools of historical, critical, linguistic, and cultural analysis have been employed by scholars of the Bible because of the important and authoritative role it has played in the Christian movement throughout history. The Bible deserves all the attention it has received from these scholars. These same scholars, however, with some notable exceptions,[2] have not always had a commitment to bringing these insights to the members of churches. They have done little to counter the popular idea that the Bible, because it belongs to an ancient pre-scientific age, cannot be taken that seriously or authoritatively by modern people.

A second reason why the Bible is viewed primarily as a sourcebook for personal piety, rather than for worldly involvement, can be attributed to the dynamics belonging to establishment religion. It will not be in the self interest of a religion such as Christianity, which has been established and still seeks to be established as the official religion of the culture, to prophetically critique the injustices to be found in that same culture. That

---

2. A few biblical scholars, such as Walter Brueggemann, Phyllis Trible, and Walter Wink among others, have shown a commitment to communicate with "ordinary Christians" without being condescending in their approach.

would set the religious community against the very culture it has courted. Therefore, in its desire to be the established religion of the culture, conventional Christianity has chosen to overlook or ignore those parts of the Bible and the teachings and acts of Jesus that, if taken seriously, form the basis for a critique of the injustices to be found in the dominant culture.

Contrary to the impression many Christians have of Church of the Crossroads, we are a church that does indeed take the Bible seriously. It has a place at the very center of our life, worship, and witness. The members of other churches and secular friends who say that we do not take the Bible very seriously may be referring to the stances and priorities that the congregation has embraced in the recent past. Included among these are the congregation's opposition to the Gulf War and the war on Iraq, its stance against oil drilling in the Arctic National Wildlife Refuge, and its outspoken support of same-sex marriage. Longtime residents of Hawai'i may be thinking of the reputation Church of the Crossroads gained, whether merited or not, when it gave sanctuary to the servicemen who were resisting the Vietnam War.

Church of the Crossroads honors that event in its history. To this day, it believes that its action arose out of its commitment to the prophetic tradition of the Bible and to Jesus who said, "Blessed are the peacemakers, for they will be called the children of God" (Matt 5:9). At the same time, the congregation has come to understand the "underside" of its action. At times, in the fervor of social witness, the feelings of those who cannot agree with a particular action are ignored. The members of Church of the Crossroads have come to understand that while the church must never relinquish its engagement with the world, which it sees as a requirement of the Gospel, it must also pay considerable attention to the nurture and care of its members. Church of the Crossroads is a far different congregation from what it was forty years ago. Today, it seeks to move towards a balance between the inner and outer dimensions of its life.

Within the congregation, one often hears members speak of the spirit of Crossroads. They understand that there is a distinctive congregational culture or spirit that informs this particular church. There was a time when they saw Church of the Crossroads as an important church within the larger culture, a theologically liberal congregation, a community of faith in which diversity was acknowledged and celebrated, and a church that was involved in the burning issues of the times. In all fairness, some of the members still view the congregation this way, and in some respects they are not mistaken.

Gradually, though, some of the ways in which the members describe their church are changing. I believe that these changing views are a direct result of the process of disestablishment. First, instead of regarding their church as an important church, that is, an influential church, many members, including myself, are becoming far more modest in the claims they make about Church of the Crossroads. Secondly, they are increasingly more apt to describe Church of the Crossroads as theologically focused, rather than as simply liberal. Thirdly, many would now acknowledge that, in addition to being a church community that is diverse in its membership, Church of the Crossroads is presently enjoying a tremendous unity (not to be confused with uniformity) in the Spirit, which has not always been true in the past. Finally, they still see the congregation as engaged in the world, but in addition they are likely to speak of the way in which its members care for one another.

One example of this last changing perception will serve to illustrate. A family that was active in the congregation during the early 1980s left the congregation and Hawai'i because of a new employment opportunity. When they returned to Hawai'i and the church a decade later, they remarked on the way in which the members of the congregation cared for older members and for one another, and that this was something they had not always observed earlier. The ethos of the congregation is now informed not only by its witness in the world, but also by its ministry of care and nurture within the community. If I were to articulate the emerging ethos of Church of the Crossroads in this time of transition, I would state it this way: *Church of the Crossroads is a Christian community modest in its ministry and mission, committed to theological reflection within the congregation, intent upon maintaining the unity of the Spirit as it celebrates the many gifts, stories, and backgrounds to be found in its diverse membership, and ready both to engage the world with the truth of the Gospel and also to encourage a ministry of care, support, and hospitality within the community itself.*

I would like to explore each of these in reverse order, beginning with the commitment Church of the Crossroads has both to a faithful witness in the world and to the care of one another within the community. For me, this commitment which partially informs the ethos of Church of the Crossroads is best illustrated in the way that the community understands the Sacrament of Holy Communion, and also the way it approaches and interprets the Sacrament of Baptism. The way in which the members and friends of Church of the Crossroads gather around the communion table and share bread and wine expresses both the commitment of its members to the well-being of one another and to the well-being of the world. The Sacrament of Baptism is the basis for the congregation's ministry both within the community and beyond the doorsteps of the church.

GATHERED AROUND THE TABLE

Following the traditional pattern of Congregationalism, the Sacrament of Holy Communion is celebrated at Church of the Crossroads on the first Sunday of each month and also at other services, including All Saints' Sunday, Thanksgiving Sunday, Christmas, Maundy Thursday, the Easter Vigil, and Pentecost Sunday. In the future, the congregation may decide to include this sacrament in every service. While it is not as yet celebrated at every service, the members of the church place much importance on this sacrament. Church attendance is slightly higher on the first Sunday of each month.

Following the "First Service of Word and Sacrament" found in *The United Church of Christ Book of Worship*, the pastor often begins the celebration with the words,

> This is the joyful feast of the people of God.
> Men and women, youth and children,
> come from the east and the west,
> from the north and south
> and gather about Christ's table.[3]

Thus, the tone of the celebration is announced. No longer seen primarily as an act of individual personal piety, although it may remain that for some, the sharing of bread and wine is now seen as a feast. Indeed, all who belong to the community, both members and friends, and also strangers are invited to the table—men, women, youth, and children. The table is open to all.

I remember the Lord's Supper in the Baptist church of my youth. All eyes were closed at certain times and when they were open, they were

---

3. Reprinted from the *Book of Worship*, © 2002 by permission of the United Church of Christ, Local Church Ministries, Worship and Education Ministry Team, Cleveland, Ohio, 44.

The Spirit of Crossroads

focused on the pastor and the deacons. Each congregant avoided eye contact with his or her co-communicants as they were seated in their pews. This is not the way it is at Church of the Crossroads. Those who gather around the table are encouraged to look at one another and embrace one another as they celebrate the sacrament.

The words that are said and the prayers that are given set the tone. The bread and wine are shared in the context of thanksgiving—thanksgiving for the creation, for the biblical heritage that has shaped the Story that continues to inform the lives of the members and their life together, for the prophets and the apostles, for "Mary, our sister," and for Jesus the Christ who lived among us, who suffered and died on the cross for our well-being and the well-being of the world, and who, on the third day was raised from death. The Prayer of Thanksgiving concludes:

> We bless you, gracious God,
> for the presence of your Holy Spirit
> in the church you have gathered.
> With your sons and daughters of faith
> in all places and times,
> we praise you with joy.[4]

The Sanctus is sung, often rhythmically, using perhaps a musical setting from another culture. Then, after the Words of Institution are given, God is asked to send the Holy Spirit "on this bread and wine, on our gifts, and on us."

> Strengthen your universal church that it may be the champion of peace and justice in all the world. Restore the earth with your grace that is able to make all things new. Be present with us as we share this meal, and throughout all our lives, that we may know you as the Holy One, who with Christ and the Holy Spirit, lives forever. Amen.[5]

On other occasions, a prayer is offered on behalf of the gathered community, that it may be as salt, yeast, and light in the world, in keeping with the scriptural passages quoted at the beginning of this chapter.

Then, all are invited to come forward and share bread and wine in the presence of Jesus the Christ and one another. Older members of the congregation are either helped to come forward or are served in their

---

4. Ibid., 46.
5. Ibid., 48.

seats. Children come forward with their parent, parents, or perhaps a teacher. Babies and small children are carried by their mothers or fathers. As each one comes forward, those who serve them call them by name and invite them to eat and drink with thanksgiving. As people return to their seats, those who desire an anointing with oil and a prayer for healing are invited to go to one of four stations located in the corners of the sanctuary. The anointing is administered and the prayers for healing are given by members of the congregation.

These words and gestures are not empty words. They say something about the commitments of those who participate in the sacrament. Through their participation in the sacrament, as members of the Body of Christ, they commit themselves to love and serve one another and to extend hospitality towards the stranger in their midst. They also commit themselves to a faithful witness in the world, knowing that the work of transformation in the world belongs not to them but to God. They come as brothers and sisters to the table, with their stories, their sorrows, and their joys. They come in hope and expectation that they will be gifted with the presence of Jesus the Christ, who is both their host and their representative and also the representative of the Holy One who in compassion moves towards them and the world.

There is an eschatological dimension, also, in this sacrament. That dimension is encompassed in the traditional words of the liturgy:

> Christ's death, O God, we proclaim.
> Christ's resurrection, we declare.
> Christ's coming we await.
> Glory be to you, O God.[6]

I confess that I do not usually include the words "Christ's coming we await" in the communion prayer, partly because I have found that they are most usually taken literally rather than metaphorically by those who hear them. In this instance, I believe that a literal interpretation betrays the metaphorical nature of the language. Even so, to say that we await Christ's coming is to say that we live with the hope that one day the promises of God will be fulfilled. Whether or not these particular words are included in the prayer, the eschatological dimension has already been alluded to in the words of the Prayer of Thanksgiving.

6. Ibid., 47.

> We bless you for the beauty of the earth
> and for the vision of the day
> when sharing by all will mean scarcity for none.[7]

What I have always sensed is that this eschatological hope for a world in which the needs of all will be met is not only *spoken* in the words surrounding the sacrament; it is also *enacted* in the sharing of the bread and wine. Around the table, *all are fed, everyone is served, and everyone receives enough.* The eschatological hope of a world in which the resources of creation will be justly distributed is already being realized in the sharing of bread and wine around the Lord's Table. In one sense, this sacrament sets us *apart* from the world and is a judgment upon the world, for what we do around the table does not represent, for the most part, what is taking place in the world. In another sense, the world and its needs have entered into the sacrament and form its context, along with the biblical accounts of all the meals Jesus shared with others.

This sacrament, then, brings together a community in which the love and care of one another is demonstrated, a community into which the stranger is welcomed, a community of justice and of hope, and a community which is then sent into the world to witness to the peace and justice of God's realm—to be as salt, yeast, and light in the world.

BAPTIZED FOR MINISTRY

I want to speak of the Sacrament of Baptism as the act that forms the basis for our ministry both within and beyond the community of faith. Along with the Sacrament of the Lord's Supper, this sacrament also shapes the ethos, the character and spirit of Church of the Crossroads as its members through their vocations serve one another in the community and enter into a faithful witness in the world.

Each time a child is baptized, the child's parent or parents are asked:

> Do you promise, by the grace of God,
> to be Christ's disciple(s),
> to follow in the way of our Savior,
> to resist oppression and evil,
> to show love and justice,

---

7. Ibid., 45.

and to witness to the work and word of Jesus Christ
as best you are able?[8]

This same question is asked of the young person who is ready to confirm his or her baptism, or of the adult who presents himself or herself for baptism. When an infant is baptized, one or both parents will have been baptized. The baptized parents must declare their own intention to fulfill the demands of discipleship. At Church of the Crossroads, we do not baptize an infant or a child unless his or her parent or parents are ready to enter a covenantal promise with the members of the church to bring up and nurture the child in the Christian faith. In this time of disestablishment, the church should not baptize children simply because it was once the expectation of the culture that everyone would be nominally Christian.

The baptismal promise to be a disciple of Christ is not to be taken lightly. It is a declaration that our work as baptized persons in the church and in the world will be carried out by the grace of God. The baptismal promise to carry forth the ministry of love, justice, and peace as Christ's disciples is also emphasized in the renewal of baptismal vows, which at Church of the Crossroads is included in the Sunday service during the Season of Epiphany when the baptism of Jesus is recalled and also in the Easter Vigil. On those occasions, the baptized are asked, "Will you strive for love, justice, and peace among all people, respecting the dignity of every human being?" Following an affirmative response, everyone is then sprinkled with water.

These baptismal promises are fulfilled in the callings (vocations) of those who belong to a community of faith as they are exercised both within the church and in the world. At Church of the Crossroads, we recognize that the ministry of all begins with our baptism. The misconception that ordination rather than baptism is the basis of ministry is still alive and well within conventional Christian circles. This misconception has had serious consequences for the church. To associate the idea of "call" only with those who are ordained serves to set the clergy apart from and above the congregation.

Certainly, the idea of "vocation" (from *vocare*, to call) as applying uniquely to clergy is a carry-over from the medieval assumption that the term refers to the call to monastic life. However, this idea was challenged when Martin Luther expanded the term to include all walks of life. In his

---

8. Ibid., 137.

The Spirit of Crossroads

1520 treatise *To the Christian Nobility of the German Nation*, Luther wrote that not only churchly authorities but also temporal authorities are called by God to a "work and office." He then went on to say that a

> ... cobbler, a smith, a peasant—each has the work and office of his trade, and yet they are all alike consecrated priests and bishops. Further, everyone must benefit and serve every other by means of his own work or office so that in this way many kinds of work may be done for the bodily and spiritual welfare of the community, just as all the members of the body serve one another.[9]

The idea that every baptized person has a vocational calling would be restored to the community of faith if baptism were to be acknowledged as the source of all ministry, whether that of the laity or the clergy.

Ministry, here, is envisioned as a faithful stewardship of all that has been entrusted to us by God, the giver of life.[10] We have been entrusted with much, not only the faith community of which we are members, but also the whole of creation and its people. The members of Church of the Crossroads have come to understand stewardship as far more than giving money to the church. Stewardship in a more profound sense is all that we do through our vocational callings. The task of stewardship, given in the beginning to the human being who is put in the Garden of Eden "to till it and keep it" (Gen 2:15), can be extended to include all of our various callings in the church and the world. Stewardship, though, is not just *something we do*; it has to do with *who we are*. We are not created to be masters but rather stewards whose limited authority in the world is a *derived* authority. It is an authority and a responsibility granted by God, the Creator of all. In the words of Brian Wren's hymn:

> We are not our own. Earth forms us,
> human leaves on nature's growing vine,
> Fruit of many generations,
> seeds of life divine. . . .
>
> Therefore let us make thanksgiving,
> and with justice, willing and aware,

---

9. Luther, "To the Christian Nobility of the German Nation," 15. Luther bases his idea on 1 Cor 12:14–26.

10. For an insightful study on the theme of stewardship and its importance for the life of Christian churches, see Hall, *The Steward: A Biblical Symbol Come of Age*, rev. ed.

> give to earth, and all things living,
> liturgies of care.[11]

Our task as stewards is to love and care for the world as God himself/herself loves and cares for the world. In baptism, we are claimed by God for this ministry.

Thus, the person who carries out a ministry of care or service within the community of faith is fulfilling his or her vocational calling. In like manner, the office worker, the teacher, the social worker, the business person, the artist, the writer, the store clerk who, through his or her vocation, serves the needs of the world is also fulfilling his or her baptismal vows as a disciple of Christ.

The movement from the reality of brokenness and despair towards hope and well-being in the lives of those who enter the doors of the church becomes possible as the members of the church engage in the ministries of listening, speaking, love, and hospitality within the church community. These gifts of ministry are made possible by the entrance of each member into the church through the act of baptism. In the same vein, it is through the vocational involvements of the members in the world, articulated as the work of discipleship made possible through baptism, that the church is able to listen to the world and enter those places in the world where the struggle between hope and despair takes place. Through the exercise of ministry both within the context of the church and in the context of the world, the church is able to maintain a creative balance between the inner and outer dimensions of its life.

In these ways, both the sacrament of the Lord's Supper and the Sacrament of Baptism shape the ethos of Church of the Crossroads. The members of the church understand their faith community as one that is concerned both with the well-being of the world and the well-being of its members. I now will discuss the theme of diversity and unity within this community of faith. The working out of the dialectic between diversity and unity has also informed the ethos of Church of the Crossroads.

DIVERSE MEMBERS, ONE SPIRIT

Church of the Crossroads is a community of faith that celebrates the diversity of its members. This diversity is evidenced in a number of ways.

---

11. Wren, "We Are Not Our Own," 1989. *The New Century Hymnal*. No. 564, © 1989 by Hope Publishing Co., Carol Stream, IL 60188. All rights reserved. Used by permission.

The Spirit of Crossroads

Founded as a multicultural congregation made up of young people from Chinese, Japanese, and other ethnic backgrounds, the congregation still encompasses a racial diversity. The percentage of Caucasian, or *haole*, members has increased over the years, and some see this as a gradual "whitening" of the congregation. However, I view this phenomenon as a reflection of the fact that Hawai'i as a whole has a far greater percentage of Caucasian residents today than it once did. Furthermore, many of the *haole* members of Church of the Crossroads are married to persons of other ethnic heritages. Many of their children and grandchildren, as are my own, are *hapa haole*, a Hawaiian term which describes persons of mixed races. Today, Church of the Crossroads includes members from Chinese, Hispanic, Japanese, Filipino, Native Hawaiian, African American, and Caucasian heritages.

There is also a diversity of ages in the membership of Church of the Crossroads. Although there is a high percentage of persons who are over the age of sixty-five, all age groups are represented in the church's membership. Regularly, the cries of babies are heard during services of worship. The porch, or *lanai*, of the church has become the place where parents and their infant children gather each Sunday morning. There, the toddlers who are not yet ready to leave their parents are free to run around. At the same time, the service can be heard and experienced by the parents through the three open doors to the sanctuary. Interestingly, these parents and children are sometimes joined by other adults who are not yet ready to enter the sanctuary, but who want to listen in to what is going on just the same. Thus, it is fair to describe Church of the Crossroads as a multi-generational community of faith.

There is also a theological diversity that is present in the congregation, but I discuss this diversity later in this chapter when I describe Church of the Crossroads' commitment to theological education within the congregation. This theological diversity is partly due to the fact that the members come from a variety of Christian backgrounds, including Roman Catholic and a number of Protestant traditions, both mainline and other. A number of members come into Church of the Crossroads after being absent from church life for many years.

In the midst of this diversity, however, there are commonly held attitudes and principles that hold the congregation together. There is a commitment to uphold the spirit and intent of the Open and Affirming and Just Peace Covenants of the church. Those who cannot agree to these do not find their way into the community in the first place. There is also a commitment to uphold one another in the congregation and to respect each other's background, life experience, and beliefs. When I use the word "belief" here, I am using it in the Old English sense of the word "be-love" from which it is derived. What we believe is what we "be-love," what we hold dear.[12]

These commitments contribute to a spirit of unity in the congregation. The members of Church of the Crossroads choose not to be divided by race, age, sexual orientation, beliefs, or mental and physical abilities. Theologically speaking, I would say that we are held together by the Spirit of God working within us.

Beyond these commonly held commitments, however, there are other factors that contribute to the spirit of unity within the community. The first of these factors has to do with leadership patterns within the congregation. Within this community, *an egalitarian spirit* is at work when it comes to leadership. One of the real blessings of this church is the absence of power brokers and controlling groups. In my experience, I have witnessed churches that are literally torn apart because of competing factions. Everyone is careful not to let this happen at Church of the Crossroads. All recognize that the church, if it is divided within, cannot possibly engage the world with any kind of conviction.

Most basically, the egalitarian spirit of leadership begins with the relationship between pastor and people. There is a real sense within Church of the Crossroads that we are in this together. This does not mean that roles are not clearly defined. The pastor of Church of the Crossroads is recognized as one who is both pastor and teacher. As pastor, then, I must see to it that a ministry of care and nurture is carried out in the community. I must also be concerned that the members of the congregation become more and more acquainted with "the Story" that must inform our life together, and that theological reflection takes place in the hearts and minds of all. There are, of course, other responsibilities that are expected of me. Yet, the roles of pastor and teacher are uppermost in the expectations of the members of the congregation. Church of the Crossroads, in its view of pastoral leadership, has done much to restore an older conception of ordained ministry that has been lost in recent years. Ordained ministers are now viewed by many churches as chief

---

12. See Smith, *Faith and Belief*, chap. 6.

executive officers who are hired under the terms of a fixed contract. In contrast, the pastor of Church of the Crossroads is *called* to be pastor and teacher. The call is an open call, which will last as long as pastor and congregation are committed to it.

Even so, the two roles of pastor and teacher do not belong exclusively to the ordained minister. There are many teachers within the congregation, and a number of them are theologically articulate persons who are often called upon to provide leadership in the teaching ministry. In like manner, there are many who engage in a ministry of care and nurture within the congregation. The newly appointed parish nurse, Liz Nelson, has encouraged this ministry. Stories which arise out of specific instances of love and care are quietly shared each time the community gathers.

This practice of shared leadership contributes to a spirit of unity within the congregation. A second factor that also encourages unity is a *consensus style of decision making*. As a result of the New Creation Initiative which has been mentioned earlier, the work of the congregation is now carried out by mission teams organized around four areas of ministry: (a) nurture and care; (b) service; (c) peace, justice, and the stewardship of creation; and (d) administration. These teams bring together thirty to forty people who meet on a weeknight once a month. Work is carried out by each of the four teams and their plans and decisions are shared with all. Recommendations that need formal approval are then referred to a Coordinating Council, made up of representatives of the four teams as well as the elected officers of the congregation. In the Coordinating Council, decisions are made only after a consensus among the members has been achieved. Issues that divide are put on hold for future consideration. In the nineteen years I have been pastor of the congregation, I can recall only one decision that was not made unanimously, and after that one decision was made, the congregation unanimously decided not to act upon it!

One might expect considerable conflict to occur in a congregation that is undergoing a process of disestablishment in its life, ministry, and witness. I want to suggest that such conflict does arise in congregations who try to ignore the fact that they are being disestablished. As these congregations try to hold on to an image of their past glory and privilege or attempt to regain the "success" they used to enjoy, they will be subject to false expectations and competing interests. Disunity may well result. Yet, when congregations embrace the process of disestablishment and become clearer about their ministry, mission, and purpose, a spirit of unity will begin to prevail.

A COMMITMENT TO THEOLOGICAL REFLECTION

Thus far, in describing the ethos of Church of the Crossroads, I have spoken of its commitment to maintaining a balance between the inner and outer dimensions of its life as a community of faith, and also of the spirit of unity that prevails in the midst of the remarkable diversity that also characterizes its membership. I will now speak of this congregation's commitment to theological reflection and education.

There is, it must be acknowledged, a tremendous diversity of theological perspectives present in the membership of Church of the Crossroads. The church has established three categories of membership. Associate Members are those who cannot in all honesty profess their faith in Jesus the Christ. They do, however, want to belong to the community as those who believe in God and who are committed to its life and ministry. A second category of membership is the Affiliate Member. These are people, such as students, who may belong to other congregations and usually live elsewhere but who wish to affiliate with Church of the Crossroads while they are living in Honolulu. Finally, Regular Members are those who have been baptized and who are led in the midst of the gathered community to profess Jesus the Christ as the "pioneer and perfecter" of their faith (Heb 12:2).

Many members of the church are associate members and this fact contributes to the theological diversity to be found in the community. Having said this, there is an understanding among all that Church of the Crossroads is a *Christian* congregation, and that, as such, it will seek to shape its life and ministry according to how it interprets the person and work of Jesus the Christ, and how the life of Jesus, especially his passion, reveals the nature of God to those who are attentive. Inasmuch as it continues to focus its attention on a theology of the cross rather than a theology of glory, God will be understood as the One who continually reveals himself/herself in the crucified Christ, a God who in compassion chooses to dwell in the midst of a creation longing for transformation. God, revealed in the cross of Christ, is for Church of the Crossroads the One who has an ongoing, abiding commitment to the creation and to the well-being of the human community. This commitment of God to the creation is a living, ongoing commitment. Truth, then, arising out of faith, is a living truth. As a living truth, it can never be fixed or something that can be finally and fully understood. It can never be finally or fully possessed. It is something that possesses us. It is something that we can only seek after, but never fully obtain.

To many Christians who want a faith that leaves no room for doubt, this notion of the truth would seem unsatisfactory. These Christians will find more satisfaction in a theology of glory that offers final answers rather than a theology of the cross that invites questions. Moreover, a theology of the cross will seem to be too negative for these Christians, and also too uncertain, simply because such a theology invites an honest look at the reality of despair and brokenness in and around us. At the same time, a theology of the cross will have the capacity to speak to Christians who want a faith that does not overlook or ignore the painful truths of human existence. Writes Douglas John Hall,

> While the theology of glory vanquishes (that is, claims to vanquish) all that negates by presenting a triumphant positive, the theology of the cross provides a basis of trust and courage enabling faith to enter more deeply into the sphere of the negative, and to *engage* it—engage, not conquer.[13]

Engaging the negative is surely a task worthy of the Gospel in our context, filled as it is with so much war, injustice, violence, and hatred. Yet, this theology of the cross, in its eschatological dimension, also looks to a positive end, to the "negation of the negation."

> The process of redemption is hidden from ordinary sight, yet it becomes visible to the eyes of faith as glimpses of fulfillment, intimations of the yes that overcomes every no. And such faith issues in the *hope* that this gracious process moves towards an end—*eschaton*—that is indeed wholly positive, though the character of *God's* positive may be entirely incommensurate with human expectation.[14]

Though the theology of the cross looks forward to a positive end, it cannot or dare not ignore the important role that the negative plays in its formation. We recall Luther's dependence upon the "way of negation" as employed in the work of Nicholas of Cusa. As employed by Nicholas, the

---

13. Hall, *The Cross in our Context*, 30.
14. Ibid., 31.

via negativa seeks to articulate the living truth of the Christian faith by stating what it is *not*. Douglas John Hall employs this when he writes about the three so-called theological virtues named by Paul in 1 Corinthians 13—faith, hope, and love.

> ... remembering the importance of the *via negativa* for both Paul and Luther, the three positive virtues should be stated together with what they negate: faith (not sight), hope (not consummation), love (not power). Without the three negations, the three positives too easily devolve into platitudes. It is necessary as always, when speaking of this tradition, to keep before one that which is ruled out—*theologia gloriae*. The theology of glory, in whatever guise it assumes, is invariably tempted to be a theology of sight, not faith; finality, not hope; and power, not love.[15]

This is a statement that all the members of the Church of the Crossroads, with all of their differences in theological perspective, could affirm. In this particular community of faith, there is a seeking after faith, not sight; hope, not finality; and love, not power. As such, this community seeks to be centered in a theology of the cross rather than a theology of glory.

This is the kind of theological reflection that engages those who belong to Church of the Crossroads. I have often described our community as one in which you don't have to park your mind at the doorstep of the church before you come in. It could also be described as a community in which faith is always in dialogue with doubt. Faith without doubt is a dead, fixed faith, a faith belonging to Christendom but not to a Christian movement.

Theological education is valued at Church of the Crossroads. Adult education classes take place each Sunday morning before the worship service. In addition, informal groups are continually organized and they gather to read and reflect upon selected books of theology or recently published works of fiction and nonfiction. Church of the Crossroads wants to have a laity that is theologically articulate. The education of the young is also encouraged. Church school classes for youngsters take place each Sunday morning. These are taught by committed, reflective members of the church who themselves are committed to their own theological education. A confirmation program for youth is also organized on a regular basis.

---

15. Ibid., 33.

The Spirit of Crossroads

Such a commitment to theological education is necessary in any Christian community that is intent upon making its way faithfully in the new context in which it finds itself. The old theology of glory, with its focus on certitude and its disdain of those who dare to question its assumptions, will no longer suffice among a people who know and accept the fact that they are being disestablished. It is the theology of the cross that can truly speak to a community willing to embrace its new position in the world. This theology of the cross, inasmuch as it speaks to the uncertainties and ambiguities of human experience, will always be willing to enter into a dialogue with doubt and will always be ready to seek new understanding. Such a theology continues to inform the ethos of Church of the Crossroads.

THEMES AND METAPHORS

Finally, I want to speak of Church of the Crossroads as a community that is marked by *modesty* in its own self-understanding of its ministry and mission. No longer does this community live under the illusion that it is important or even significant in the eyes of the world. It knows itself as a community that is more and more being moved to the periphery of the culture that surrounds it. This is simply a fact of its existence. It does not see itself as participating nor does it want to participate in the new conservative Christian majority that has gained prominence in the United States in recent years. Rather, it is a community that is beginning to give thanks that it is no longer at the center of the culture.

There are certain themes and metaphors that are becoming important for this community as it finds itself redefining its ministry in the new context in which it finds itself. These themes and metaphors are helping the members of Church of the Crossroads to speak of the spirit or ethos of their congregation.

First is the theme of *empire*. It has become evident to many observers of the political, social, and cultural life of the United States that this nation is best described as an empire. Even those who are now in power in the United States are using the image of empire to describe the nation. We recall what a senior advisor to President Bush said to Ron Suskind, a writer of current affairs: "We're an empire now, and when we act, we create our own reality."[16] It has also become evident that there is a religious

---

16. Suskind, "Without a Doubt," *New York Times Magazine* (October 17, 2004), 51.

underpinning to America's view of itself as an empire that can be located in the cultural Christianity and in the theology of glory that has informed its history. The God who is great and powerful has made America great and powerful.

Although this notion of empire for the most part receives no critique from churches belonging to the Christian right, there are a number of Christian minorities within all the churches who are viewing this development as incompatible with biblical faith. The importance of these minorities for the future faithfulness of the Christian Movement cannot be underestimated. They represent a new kind of *diaspora*, a scattering, a separation from the churches of conventional American Christianity. As I described in the first chapter of this book, all Christian churches really belong to a diaspora, whether they realize it or not.[17] These Christian minorities, then, represent a particular diaspora within a larger diaspora. The difference between them and the churches of conventional American Christianity is that they are embracing their diaspora status and discovering in it a new identity and a new relationship with the world. These church communities are important to the future of the Christian faith, for they represent the possibility of a much needed reformation of Christianity. It is a hopeful sign that prophetic and critical voices still arise from Christian churches and are heard. Significant minority communities such as Sojourners, the Open Door Community of Atlanta, Church of our Savior in Washington, DC, Church of the Crossroads, and numerous other communities of faith are to be found throughout the United States. These communities understand the incompatibility between empire and biblical faith, and their witness will not be silenced.

In the context of the empire that is the United States of America, Church of the Crossroads has found meaning in the themes of *exile* and *restoration* that are at the center of the prophetic writings associated with the Babylonian Exile of the sixth century BCE. During that time, the people of Israel found themselves living in the context of empire as an exiled people. This is not unlike the way communities such as Church of the Crossroads see themselves today. In many of his books, Walter Brueggemann has written extensively on the themes of exile and restoration as he has described the experience of those sixth-century exiles and the corresponding experience of the mainline Protestant congregations

---

17. See my discussion under "A Church of a Diaspora," chap. 1.

who are now facing the fact and challenge of their disestablishment. As did the exiled community of the sixth century BCE and the Jewish community throughout its subsequent history, these churches of mainline Protestantism who are being exiled to the edge of the society will surely experience the struggle between despair and hope and no small amount of uncertainty and awkwardness as they make their way through the time of their re-formation. In faith, they may choose to anticipate a kind of restoration, but their new life will not look anything like their old existence, any more than the exiles of the sixth century BCE who returned to Jerusalem and a ruined temple could expect the new shape of their religious life to resemble what they had known in the past.

In his book, *Cadences of Home*, Brueggemann summarizes the particular tasks that belong to communities who understand themselves as communities in exile in the midst of empire. These practices will not be comfortable and safe, but filled with danger, for they may well set the faith communities that practice them against the empire that seeks to co-opt them. Brueggemann names six practices of hope and resistance.

> *Dangerous memories* reaching all the way back to our barren mother Sarah.
> *Dangerous criticism* that mocks the deadly empire.
> *Dangerous promises* that imagine a shift of power in the world.
> *Dangerous songs* that sing of unexpected newness of life.
> *Dangerous bread* free of all imperial ovens; all leading to
> *Dangerous departures* of heart and body and mind, leavings undertaken in trust and obedience.[18]

These tasks are in one sense modest tasks, but they are tasks that require both courage and intentionality. They are also tasks that will continue to inform and shape the ethos of communities such as Church of the Crossroads.

There is yet another way to describe both the identity and the tasks of congregations who understand themselves as communities that are being disestablished and who seek to be faithful embodiments of the spirit of a Christian movement that existed before Christendom and that must be rediscovered anew in the present. The images of salt, light, and yeast that we find in three sayings of Jesus may be used to describe the life and

---

18. Brueggemann, *Cadences of Home*, 134.

ministry of such congregations.[19] In these sayings, salt, light, and yeast function as metaphors. According to the *American Heritage Dictionary of the English Language,* 4th edition, a metaphor is "a figure of speech in which a word or phrase that ordinarily designates one thing is used to designate another, thus making an implicit comparison."[20]

In a metaphoric way, then, a community of faith may be described as salt, yeast, and light. These are surely modest images for the church. Salt is a hidden ingredient that gives taste to the whole. Likewise, yeast, when hidden in the flour, causes the dough to rise. Light is a more visible element, but the light referred to in the saying of Jesus is a small household lamp that nonetheless is able to give light to all in the house. It too is a modest image.

These are the modest images that describe the church as it enters into a relationship with the world, when it becomes involved in the life of the world, when it bears witness to the peace and justice that belong to God's mission, *missio dei.* In the eyes of a world enamored with bigness and success, the witness belonging to salt, yeast and a little light may seem insignificant. Yet, what would food taste like without salt? What would happen to bread baked without yeast? How would one see in a darkened house without the aid of a lamp? The witness of the church is far from insignificant! Yet, there is a modesty that is called for in the witness of a church that must acknowledge the abuses of its Christendom past even as it seeks to be faithful in the present. Moreover, in a theology of the cross, there can be little room for grand images that speak of success and achievement. A church whose life and ministry and whose ethos is shaped by the cross can be nothing less nor anything more than salt mixed in with food, the small lamp giving light to all in a household, or yeast mixed with the flour.

So may the prayer of Christian communities who wish to move beyond their Christendom past and who are ready to embrace their awkward present, even as they place their hope in the Spirit's leading towards a future that is not yet disclosed, be the prayer that is included in the communion liturgy of the "Service of Word and Sacrament II," *United Church of Christ Book of Worship.*

---

19. Matt 5:13–16; Lk 13:18–19.

20. *American Heritage Dictionary of the English Language,* 4th Edition, Houghton Mifflin Company, 2000.

The Spirit of Crossroads

Gracious God,
we ask you to bless
this bread and cup and all of us
with the outpouring of your Holy Spirit.
Through this meal,
make us the body of Christ,
the church,
your servant people,
that we may be salt, and light, and leaven
for the furtherance of your will
in all the world.
Amen.[21]

---

21. Reprinted from the *Book of Worship*, © 2002 by permission of the United Church of Christ, Local Church Ministries, Worship and Education Ministry Team, Cleveland, Ohio, 71–72.

Bibliography

American Heritage Dictionary of the English Language. 4th ed. Houghton Mifflin Company, 2000.

Anon. "*De Colores.*" In *The New Century Hymnal.* Cleveland, OH: The Pilgrim Press, 1995.

———. "How Can I Keep from Singing?" *Bright Jewels for the Sunday School,* ed. Robert Lowrey, New York, 1869. In *The New Century Hymnal.* Cleveland, OH: The Pilgrim Press, 1995.

Beach, Curtis. "O How Glorious, Full of Wonder." In *The New Century Hymnal.* Cleveland, OH: The Pilgrim Press, 1995.

Berry, Wendell. *A Place on Earth.* New York: North Point Press, 1983.

Bettenson, Henry, ed. *Documents of the Christian Church.* London: Oxford University Press, 1943.

———. *Documents of the Christian Church.* 2d ed. London: Oxford University Press, 1963.

Bonhoeffer, Dietrich. *The Cost of Discipleship.* New York: Simon & Schuster, Touchstone Edition, 1995.

———. *Letters and Papers from Prison: The Enlarged Edition.* Translated by Reginald Fuller, Frank Clark, et al. London: SCM, 1953.

Brueggemann, Walter. *Cadences of Home.* Louisville: John Knox Press, 1997.

———, ed. *Hope for the World.* Louisville: Westminster John Knox Press, 2001.

———. *Israel's Praise: Doxology Against Idolatry and Ideology.* Philadelphia: Fortress Press, 1988.

Church of the Crossroads. "1923 Church Covenant." Honolulu, rev. 1992.

———. "Fifth Anniversary Brochure." 1928. Church of the Crossroads archives, Honolulu.

———. "Just Peace Covenant." Adopted March, 1992. Honolulu.

———. "The New Creation Initiative." Adopted January, 2003. Honolulu.

———. "The Open and Affirming Covenant." Adopted March 8, 1992. Honolulu.

———. "Study Paper." February, 1969. Church of the Crossroads archives, Honolulu.

———. "Twentieth Anniversary Brochure." 1943. Church of the Crossroads archives, Honolulu.

Clyde, Arthur G., ed. *The New Century Hymnal.* Cleveland, OH: The Pilgrim Press, 1995.

Cochrane, Arthur. *The Church's Confession under Hitler.* Philadelphia: Westminster Press, 1962.

Commanger, Henry Steele, ed. *Documents of American History.* 8th ed. New York: Appleton-Century-Crofts, 1968.

Consultation on Common Texts. *The Revised Common Lectionary.* Nashville, TN: Abingdon Press, 1993.

Bibliography

Dallaire, Roméo. *Shake Hands with the Devil*. Toronto: Random House Canada, 2003.
Donne, John. *Devotions*. Ann Arbor: The University of Michigan Press, 1959.
Eck, Diana. *A New Religious America*. San Francisco: Harper Collins Publishers, 2001.
Fuchs, Lawrence H. *Hawaii Pono: A Social History*. New York: Harcourt, Brace & World, Inc., 1961.
Hall, Douglas John. *Confessing the Faith*. Minneapolis: Fortress Press, 1996.
———. *The Cross in Our Context*. Minneapolis: Fortress Press, 2003.
———. *God and Human Suffering*. Minneapolis: Fortress Press, 1986.
———. *Professing the Faith*. Minneapolis: Fortress Press, 1993.
———. *The Reality of the Gospel and the Unreality of the Churches*. Philadelphia: Westminster Press, 1976.
———. *The Steward: A Biblical Symbol Come of Age*. Rev. ed. Eugene, OR: Wipf and Stock Publishers, 2004.
Hanh, Thich Nhat. *Living Buddha, Living Christ*. New York: Riverhead Books, 1995.
Hemphill, Betty and Robert F. Hemphill. *The Crossroads Witness*. Honolulu: Church of the Crossroads, 1988.
Hine, Stuart K. "How Great Thou Art." Pacific City, OR: Manna Music, Inc. 1953.
Ho, Elsie. "Interview, March 29, 1982." Church of the Crossroads archives, Honolulu.
Holloway, Richard. *Doubts and Loves*. Edinburgh: Canongate Books, 2001.
Honolulu Star-Bulletin. Editorial. March 12, 1969.
Kenseth, Arnold. *Sabbaths, Sacraments, and Seasons*. Amherst, MA: Windhover Press, 1982.
Kierkegaard, Søren. *The Sickness Unto Death*. Translated by Howard V. Hong and Edna H. Hong. Princeton, NJ: Princeton University Press, 1980.
Lind, Andrew. "Letter to Moderator Teruo Sasaki." March, 1978. Church of the Crossroads archives, Honolulu.
Lull, Timothy F., ed. *Martin Luther's Basic Theological Writings*. Minneapolis: Fortress Press, 1989.
Luther, Martin. "To the Christian Nobility of the German Nation." In *Luther's Works*. Philadelphia: Fortress Press, 1970.
Mead, Loren A. *The Once and Future Church*. Bethesda, MD: Alban Institute, 1991.
Molefe, S. C. "Amen, siyakudumisa." arr. Dave Dargie, from the *Lumko Institute Songbook*, in *The New Century Hymnal*. Cleveland, OH: The Pilgrim Press, 1995.
Moltmann, Jürgen. *The Crucified God: The Cross of Christ as the Foundation and Criticism of Christian Theology*. Translated by R. A. Wilson and John Bowden. Philadelphia: Fortress Press, 1974.
Postman, Neil. *Amusing Ourselves to Death: Public Discourse in the Age of Show Business*. New York: Penguin Books, 1985.
Rahner, Karl. *Mission and Grace: Essays on Pastoral Theology*, Vol. 1. Translated by Cecily Hastings. London: Sheed and Ward, 1963.
Rantala, Judy. "Living Between the Ideal and the Actual." Essay on church's history. Honolulu: Church of the Crossroads, 1998.
Rayson, Delwyn R. "Church Document." October, 1960. Church of the Crossroads archives, Honolulu.
———. *Faith in a World Come of Age*. Honolulu: Church of the Crossroads, 1961.
———. "Fiftieth Anniversary Sermon." May 20, 1973. Church of the Crossroads archives, Honolulu.

Bibliography

―――. "Jesus and the Beatles—Or, Where Do We Go From Here." A sermon, August 21, 1966. Church of the Crossroads archives, Honolulu.

―――. "Letter to Congregation." January 8, 1964. Church of the Crossroads archives, Honolulu..

―――. "A Statement to the Congregation on The Coffee House." June 13, 1965. Church of the Crossroads archives, Honolulu.

Robinson, Anthony B. "Identity and Pluralism at The Crossroads." A paper for discussion. November 18, 1985. Church of the Crossroads archives, Honolulu.

Smith, Wilfred Cantwell. *Faith and Belief*. Princeton, NJ: Princeton University Press, 1979.

Suskind, Ron. "Without a Doubt." In *New York Times Magazine,* October 17, 2004.

Taylor, Barbara Brown. *Speaking of Sin*. Cambridge, MA: Cowley Publications, 2000.

Tillich, Paul. *The Courage to Be*. New Haven, CT: Yale University Press, 1952.

United Church of Christ. *The Book of Worship of the United Church of Christ*. New York: Office for Church Life and Leadership, 1986.

Wallis, Jim. "A New Confession of Christ." Washington, DC: Sojourners. Statement published October, 2004. http://www.sojo.net.

Weaver, Galen. "Letter to Theodore Richards, May 2, 1927." Church of the Crossroads archives, Honolulu.

Weil, Simone. *Waiting for God*. Translated by Emma Craufurd. New York: Harper Collins Publishers, 2001.

Williams, Roger. Citation from his trial in First Liberty Institute. *Living With Our Deepest Differences*. Nashville, TN: Freedom Forum First Amendment Center, n.d.

Wren, Brian. "Here Hangs a Man Discarded." In *Faith Renewed*. Carol Stream, IL: Hope Publishing Company, 1995.

―――. "May the Sending One Defend You." In *The New Century Hymnal*. Cleveland, OH: The Pilgrim Press, 1995.

―――. "We Are Not Our Own." In *The New Century Hymnal*. Cleveland, OH: The Pilgrim Press, 1995.

Wright, Ronald. *A Short History of Progress*. Toronto: House of Anansi Press Inc., 2004.

Yeats, William Butler. *The Collected Poems of W. B. Yeats*. Rev. 2d. ed. Edited by Richard J. Finneran. New York: Simon & Schuster, Inc., 1996.

www.ingramcontent.com/pod-product-compliance
Lightning Source LLC
Chambersburg PA
CBHW062002180426
43198CB00036B/2142